Telling Tales

D1534887

JOHN FRASER

Collins Toronto

First published 1986
by Collins Publishers
100 Lesmill Road, Don Mills, Ontario

Canadian Cataloguing in Publication Data

Fraser, John, 1944-
  Telling tales

ISBN 0-00-217641-6

1. Canada — Biography.   2. Canada — Biography — Anecdotes, facetiae, satire, etc. I. Title.

FC25.F73 1986   920'.071   C86-094241-4
F1005.F72 1986

Printed and bound in Canada

CONTENTS

For my wife

INTRODUCTION

Telling Tales owes its genesis to fate and inspiration: fate in the form of a chaotic career in Canadian journalism, and inspiration in the form of John Aubrey's wonderful pen sketches of his illustrious seventeenth-century contemporaries, known collectively as *Brief Lives*.

Aubrey was an antiquary and writer who lived between 1625 and 1697 and thus had a life set against some of the greatest events in English history. He was a young man when Charles I was executed in 1649 after a decade of civil war and its attendant political and religious strife. In 1660, when the monarchy was restored under Charles II, he was still only 35 and had great plans to shore up his sagging fortunes and to write his name among the literary worthies of his age and land.

It was these plans that endeared Aubrey to me when I first stumbled across his writings at university. Any man who could so successfully and consistently invest whatever meagre funds he had from time to time in exactly the wrong place, who could take on so many projects simultaneously that he hardly ever managed to finish one of them, who was such an easy touch for even more insolvent relatives and friends, and who — at "the merest invitation" — could while away countless hours in conversation and other unproductive pastimes in the company of warm hearts and argumentative souls: well, that is a man after my own heart. It has not been a question of trying to emulate him, but simply one of having walked along the well-traversed rut of great intentions and lesser results.

Aubrey's most admirable trait was his love of people. There was nothing so important that he could not be diverted by the promise of amicable camaraderie and tales of so and so or such and such. He had a classic journalist's mentality, epitomized by his wide and insatiable curiosity and his desire to understand what goes on at the centre of swirling events or national institutions and yet preserve a safe passageway out from either complicity or commitment.

1

When he died, it was no different than when he lived. His "estate" was an utter shambles with unpaid debts scattered about like autumn leaves in Epping Forest, scattered in fact with the same abandon as a couple of dozen uncompleted manuscripts. Over the years, more sensible folk have tried to put some order to Aubrey's chaos and to them we owe the present form of *Aubrey's Brief Lives*. In an older age, they were also known as *Minutes of Lives* in order to explain their sometimes inexplicable terseness. This was evidently not by design. Aubrey would begin to take notes on a designated Worthy Figure and, depending on the sources of his information, it could end up as a self-contained miniature masterpiece, perfectly encapsulating a leading figure's life; or, then again, it might simply be one or two anecdotes. For reasons we can only guess at, he was never able to return to the subject.

There are other oddities to his *Brief Lives* that are regarded with fulsome affection by his admirers. He had, for example, an occasional tendency to be diverted mid-essay. Thus he might begin a pen sketch of Archbishop Laud's chaplain and end up discoursing on some doctrinal heresy, quite forgetting to ever return to the subject he was ostensibly writing about. In the same way, a peripheral or perhaps more interesting character in one of his sketches could also lead him completely astray and, just when we thought we were reading about a notable Fellow of All Soul's College in Oxford, we would find ourselves following a long and passionate description of his third cousin, twice removed. He has bequeathed his imitators delightful licence to stray far away from main points.

Above all, though, in his *Brief Lives* Aubrey was fascinated by the mighty folk of his age and nation. Since he had a taste for unusual or unexpected vignettes, these figures come down to us through him not as high Pooh-Bahs, but as mortal men and women whose foibles and superstitions, generosities of spirit or eccentricities, hugely embellish the rather lifeless images we usually get from more orthodox accounts.

Whether he knew these figures personally or not, he liked nearly all of them, liked them not despite their foibles but *because* of them. It is this sturdy affection for his fellow human beings, in all their variety, that gives so much texture to his sketches. It is true he did not shy away from depicting ogres, but even here it is impossible not to sense the fascination he felt for them, as if he were describing a more sinister side of himself, or all of us.

Journalism is not an orderly profession, so there could be few greater models — even in the latter half of the twentieth century — for a journalist, than John Aubrey. I have often been comforted by the example of his disorder and haphazardness, no more so than during the writing of this book, which has been agonizingly spread out over several years and various assignments for the *Globe and Mail*. (Even now I hear the swelling chorus of employer, agent, publisher and wife singing "And so say all of us".) Life has been lived on the run. The sketch of Madame Vanier, for example, was written in New Delhi after a ghastly day of counting Sikh corpses; that of Dr. Norman Endicott in Athens during a boisterous Greek election; that of Allan Fotheringham (perhaps appropriately) in Brighton two days after the IRA tried to blow up Prime Minister Margaret Thatcher and most of the British cabinet.

The selection of victims in *Telling Tales* is a bit odd, I admit, but it is a fair reflection of the people I came up against during the first 40 years of my life. To be educated in private schools in Ontario and then at a university in Newfoundland is not normal. It may not even be sensible. To go from the overnight police desk at the old Toronto *Telegram* to the post of music and dance critic is absurd. This, however, was merely preparation for the switch from a dance and theatre critic at the *Globe and Mail* to being its eighth resident correspondent in the People's Republic of China. There are no particular explanations for this, it is just the way it has been so far, no doubt aided by my horror of saying *No* to any bizarre appointment.

The only unifying element has been the newspaper business itself, which I remain hooked to despite all the warnings of Marshall McLuhan and the example of Gordon Sinclair. It is still a good profession, maybe better than it has ever been, although it is now held in low repute by many. For me, it is life itself — not because of the infinite variety of the day, after the last edition — but because of the opportunity to share in the infinite variety of people. Journalists know better than any media critic the perils of their business, the tendency towards cynicism about the Mighty, seen too close and for too long; and the obverse tendency towards callousness with lesser fry who can be deployed for colour or back-up quotes, when and if necessary. Understanding the tendency does not mean a good journalist succumbs to it. In fact, I don't know any good journalists who aren't as naive as three-year-olds (hence their unending capacity to be genuinely shocked by political duplicity) and as ruthless as Grandma Moses. I am not talking here about the performances they put on to impress or convince either themselves or their subjects. Even less am I talking about some of the cynical and callous things they can write. When you push them to a wall, however, my experience has been that they are hopeless victims of facts and normal human emotions, and that this governs their lives more than anything else.

The same is true with the people depicted in this book. In certain instances, I have tried to take very familiar names and place them in an unfamiliar setting. In other cases, I have allowed myself an Aubreyesque luxury and gone off the deep end entirely or ended up writing about someone else. When I started work on Telling Tales, I thought it would be extremely clever to adopt formally some of Aubrey's chaos; during the course of its creation, I discovered that all the sidetrips and diversions arose almost too naturally for comfort. The criteria of choice was simple: those picked had to be Canadian; they had to be living at the time of writing; and any incident or anecdotal material had to be something I had seen or had direct access to, in some way.

4

It will become apparent during the reading of this book that it is also something of my not always humble reporter's life and for this I apologize. I do not believe there is such a thing as "objective journalism." The phrase itself is one of the great frauds of our time. There is the need to struggle towards fairness and balance, the obligation to make known any particular bias (if a journalist even knows what particular biases he is ruled by), the struggle for an appropriate prose style: all these, and more, are crucial elements in decent journalism, but they do not constitute objectivity. Not even the spare, lean style of a news agency report — so often cited within the profession as genuinely objective — constitutes objectivity: even there facts are sifted and chosen, then ranked from lead paragraphs to the final choppable sentences, according to ordinary fallible human perceptions.

There is such a thing, though, as *open* journalism, in which the practitioner does not try to hide himself behind a mask of self-serving "professionalism" or dissimulating disinterest. To write and publish stories about someone, about anyone, is not only to invade their lives; it also makes you culpable for whatever distance may exist between your perceptions of your subjects and the way they see themselves. There is no escaping this responsibility, any more than public figures can escape being written about and analyzed. Like journalists, they have eschewed anonymity and have become part of a larger family that merits inspection because they have entered everyones' lives.

JEANNE SAUVÉ

Right Honourable Jeanne Sauvé, PC, CC, CMM, CD, DHL, DS, LLD. Governor General since 1984. Born 26 April 1922 in Prud'-Homme, Saskatchewan. Educated at Notre-Dame du Rosaire Convent, University of Ottawa and the University of Paris. Assistant to the Youth Director at UNESCO in Paris from 1950-51. From 1952 to 1972, established a successful career as a freelance journalist and broadcaster. First elected to the House of Commons in October, 1972, for the Montreal riding of Ahuntsic as a Liberal and was soon appointed Minister of State for Science and Technology. In 1974 she became Minister of Environment and one year later Minister of Communications. Her appointment as Speaker of the House of Commons marked the first time a woman had been chosen for that job. Married, with one son. Roman Catholic.

During the course of her short career as Speaker of the House of Commons, Mme. Sauvé — perhaps out of blind nostalgia for her former career as a journalist — was incautious enough not only to attend the annual Ottawa *débâcle* known as the Press Gallery Dinner, but followed this up by lingering at the dangerously inebriated reception the Press Club itself tenders in the early hours of the morning.

A solitary bastion of sober and dignified respectability at an event where decorum had been dispatched to inglorious exile hours before, Mme. Sauvé found herself having to fend off the unsolicited amorous advances of the most rotund media hack on Parliament Hill. Normally a perfect gentleman, on this occasion he was a porcine rake with sweat wreathing his brow. In quick succession, he nestled close to the elegant Speaker, whispered "Jeanne, Jeanne . . ." in her ear, and placed a pudgy paw firmly on her *derrière*.

"Mr. D—! Mr. D—!" exclaimed the startled and vaguely amused future châtelaine of Rideau Hall, as she turned smartly on her heel and out of his clutches. "You and I must work very hard to preserve our little share of dignity."

EDWARD SCHREYER

Right Honourable Edward Richard Schreyer CC, CMM, CD, MA. High Commissioner to Australia since 1984. Born 21 December 1935 in Beauséjour, Manitoba. Former Governor General and former Premier of Manitoba. Educated at Beauséjour Collegiate, United College (Winnipeg) and the University of Manitoba. In 1958, he became the youngest person to be elected to the Manitoba legislature. In 1965 he became a university teacher but three years later ran successfully for the House of Commons. Resigning his federal seat in 1968, he became leader of Manitoba's New Democratic Party and presided over the government there for nearly a decade. He was the 1975 winner of the Vanier Award as "outstanding Young Canadian of the year." His appointment as Governor General commenced in 1979. Married, with two sons and two daughters.

Does anyone care anymore who on earth is Governor General of Canada? A few romantics and a few snobs perhaps, but for the most part the office of the Queen's Representative and the *de facto* Head-of-State has been allowed to dwindle into an irrelevancy that will, in all likelihood, be the last step before the job becomes extinct. The scenario is so easy to see: governors general will be transformed into constitutional presidents; the Dominion will be declared a republic; and a tenuous monarchical link — to soothe the old folks in the Atlantic provinces — will be maintained, sort of, by remaining in the moribund Commonwealth. It may happen within five years, or maybe it will take 25, but the pattern is set and there seems little inclination to change it.

The pattern takes two forms. First, the monarchical link has been systematically downgraded. We tolerate irregular visits from the Queen, but tend increasingly to fuss about the obvious anomalies and absurdities in the title Queen of Canada, rather than glorifying them and turning them on their heads to make them an adornment (even beloved eccentricities) to the nation. Our tenuous grasp of history leads us to accept, without question, that the monarchy is a divisive institution because it has nothing to do with Quebec (or conversely, and perversely, some cling to the *British* throne precisely because it does seem to irritate Quebec), forgetting entirely the stabilizing and protective role the throne played in Quebec's post-Conquest history. Who is the greatest Canadian royalist today? You won't find him or her on Parliament Hill or the Anglican Church. He's Père Jacques Monet, the eminent French-Canadian Jesuit historian, now the head of Regis College at the University of Toronto. It is his honest, lucid reading of our history that has led him to champion something that most of his colleagues consider irrational, romantic and bizarre.

The trouble is that one lone theologian and the tattered ranks of the Monarchist League can't keep the show going against a presiding philosophy which holds that we have outgrown the link to the throne and its embarrassing reminder of a colonial past. We want our constitutional profile to be smooth and bland, free from all irregularities and peculiarities; the better to hide behind encroaching facelessness.

The second form the pattern takes is the nature of the appointments to Rideau Hall. The governor general's post is now simply part of the prime minister's vast pool of political patronage. It is a useful place to dispose of the undisposable. No real attempt is made any more to let the post evolve in a genuinely interesting way. Today, there is as much chance of renewing Rideau Hall as there is of ringing in reform for the Senate. We are talking about a *fait accompli*, for it is almost inconceivable to think of a Canadian prime minister who would have the courage and wisdom to appoint a governor general who might actually attempt to drag Canadians — or simply point the direction — out of our slough of mediocre despond and act as both conscience and goad to the country.

As a symbol of this dreary but apparently acceptable transition, Ed Schreyer was almost heaven-sent. A good and decent man, the remaining Ruritanian trappings of the office were repugnant to him and he rarely bothered to do more than go through the motions. An active politician with a reputation for fair play and moderation during his time as the New Democratic Party's premier in Manitoba, he began his sojourn at Rideau Hall by announcing that he was finally going to have the time to read all of the *Encyclopedia Britannica*. Now there were those who thought this was a sure sign that he didn't intend to do anything but play cribbage and natter at tea parties; but, ever the optimist, I was rather hoping he would plough his way through to Volume XI and the splendid chapter on "Sacred Roles and Duties," in which the most primitive concepts of kingship and chieftanship are traced right through the entire human record to the present secular age. I even had hopes that he might turn into a browser and skip all the guff from Volumes I to X and get straight to the heart of the dilemma he seemed to be facing.

No such luck. The problem for Ed — I wouldn't want to embarrass him by calling him His Excellency — was that in the world of practical politics he understood so well, there was neither time nor inclination to consider the mysteries and wisdom of symbolism; and the office he was handed, beyond the basic constitutional precepts he swore to uphold and carry out, has almost entirely to do with symbolism. Action in party politics comes down to policy, legislation and enforcement. Action in vice-regal symbolism is infinitely more difficult but potentially more effective. It is all bound up in suggestion, example, constancy, aspiration and the longing, deep within all of us, to see our gravest fears and highest hopes safely personified in a worthy individual who is not better than us but instead represents what is best *in* us.

It sounds like theoretical nonsense, I know, but in fact our governors general are the beneficiaries of a delicately-wrought compromise worked out over many years in the United Kingdom between the inevitable aspirations of a democratic and egalitarian thrust to history and the lingering, still potent, craving for the nobility of leadership. Even when kings and emperors wielded unlimited power, it was precisely the sort of events — state occasions, public outings, official receptions — that constitutional monarchs and their representatives still do, that established the old despots' connections to the people and built their reputations. The balance between folksiness and sentimentality on the one side, and aloofness and pomposity on the other, defines how we regard the Pooh Bahs set above us. Vincent Massey, for example, was the first native-born Canadian to be appointed governor general and, in aping his British predecessors rather too much, he erred on the side of aloofness. Alternatively, some of the jokers who managed to get appointed as lieutenant-governors in the provinces blissfully scuttled the few remaining vestiges of dignity in their offices under the mistaken belief that this would bring them "closer to the people" or make their jobs "more relevant."

Mr. Schreyer managed to avoid either of these pitfalls by embracing a third route in which he eschewed symbolism altogether and opted to become a kind of supreme remittance man to the nation, clinging to the proferred sinecure to keep him out of trouble. In the course of various jobs for the *Globe and Mail*, I kept stumbling across him as he went about his work, starting in the early days when he clearly thought he had walked into some sort of bizarre children's party in which he was cast as Mr. Dressup, to his final days when it emerged that he rather fancied the due respect and appurtenances of the office.

ACT ONE: The Parliamentary Dining Room at the annual Press Gallery Dinner. (These rather boozy occasions are apparently not supposed to be reported, presumably to protect all the guilty, but I never signed anything.)

The Governor General is speaking. The tradition is that the speeches are all to be in a light-hearted vein and even Mr.

Massey always rose to the spirit of the moment. Four years into his office, Ed hadn't figured that spirit out yet. During his first appearance at one of these affairs, he tried sucking up to the press with what was essentially a politician's plea for favourable coverage. The gist of his message was that he was a vital, important and producing human being who had been given a flunkie's job, so please everyone be understanding. When he was invited back to speak again, he chastised the press for not respecting his office and treating him as a flunkie. I sat at a table next to the one where the Italian ambassador was sitting. Someone made a wisecrack — smart-ass interjections are also part of this curious evening's traditions — and Ed took immediate offence. Someone threw a bun in the general direction of the Governor General. Not nice, of course, but it happened.

"If anyone tries that again, I'll stop my speech," says Ed.

Guess what happened?

Of course. It rained buns and sugar cubes and before he turned into a gâteau St. Honoré, Ed was threatening to take at least once miscreant into a corridor and fight it out, man to man. The Italian ambassador was shedding real tears and his head was in his hands as he sobbed. "This can't be happening," he said over and over again. In English and Italian.

The members of the Fourth Estate, obviously, were behaving like louts, but it struck more than a few of the less inebriated scribes that they had witnessed an historic moment. The lack of respect for the man reinforced the irrelevancy of his work. The very last shreds of respect for an office that should have evolved into a unifying and enhancing focus for a fractured nation had been snapped among the very people who would largely be reporting and analysing that office — or not, as it usually turned out.

ACT TWO: The Throne Room and Gardens, Rideau Hall during one of the regular investitures for citizens who have won bravery medals.

Ed and his wife Lily now do this sort of thing not badly. He

12

has eventually settled for bland pomposity at these occasions, but a bit of formal stiffness doesn't sit badly on him as he pins medals on eagle scouts, shopkeepers, junior police officers, mothers — the usual variety of ordinary people who, through fate, have been caught out at a moment in life when they had to risk their own lives if others were to be saved.

These ceremonies are not unmoving, especially in an age which essentially doubts courage and expresses amazement not at deeds done but why people bothered to do them. The medal winners have no explanations, really. They can't tell you why they acted and others stood around, what impulse sent them into a fire or any icy river at the shout of help, what made them lunge for a gun during a robbery while someone else cowered. They are grateful that they were able to act as they did and they are proud of the medal they are receiving, but the reason why remains steadfastly elusive.

Afterwards, during a reception in the gardens, there is only one person who is clearly uncomfortable and that is Mr. Ed. He is bored with other people's small talk and infinitely boring with his own. To one young girl, who took on a killer twice her size to prevent the murder of a third person in Prince Edward Island, he has a fatherly admonishment: lie low the next time, you might get hurt. To an older man whose question to his Governor General was evidently considered unworthy, he simply turned away and looked for someone more interesting to talk to. We are not here examining *noblesse oblige* but something perilously close to *noblesse oublie*. Volume XI of the *Encyclopedia Britannica*, had he got to it, would have told him that historically the closest bond established between a king and one of his subjects was when unordinary acts of courage performed by ordinary people were publicly honoured.

ACT THREE: Some bunker of the mind in Rideau Hall during the Manitoba language crisis of 1983.

Constitutional governors general, like their monarchs, have given up most of their temporal powers, but it is not true that they have given up their real powers. These are held in reserve.

And by real powers I do not mean those well-rehearsed rights "to advise and caution," but the symbolic resources bequeathed by ancient notions of leadership and which, under the parliamentary system, are supposed to reside in either the hereditary or appointed leader of the state. With kings themselves, we have some shining examples during this century: Spain's Juan Carlos defying a military coup, or Denmark's Christian wearing the Star of David on his own breast pocket the day after the Nazi occupiers of his country ordered the rounding up of local Jews.

Such stupendously dramatic and dangerous scenes, happily, do not fall to Canadian governors general, but we nevertheless have our little moments when it would be useful to see a leader point a way to a better direction. During Ed's days of glory, there was really only one crisis which erupted that needed an adroit and humane gesture. Ironically, it occurred in his own province. The language crisis, though, went far beyond the fears of Manitoba citizens that French was going to be rammed down their throats by federal fiat. It evoked the whole canker inside the Canadian confederation that goes right back to the gallows from which Louis Riel swung. It was a cue, if ever there was one, for a governor general to walk on to centre stage. To do what? Good question and one for which there is no precise answer. In the bunker Ed retreated to, we had one message via a press secretary that His Excellency hoped Canadians would not tarnish all Manitobans with the label "bigot." Maybe he didn't have to say anything, but instead arrange to be in Manitoba doing the ordinary round of vice-regal activities just to remind people there that they were part of a larger entity. Maybe he should have tried something in Quebec or New Brunswick to remind non-Manitobans that this was a national problem where no one's record was particularly shining. There were a thousand reasons for doing nothing, from possible constitutional impropriety to personal timidity, but there was not one excuse.

A decade and a half earlier, an old man sick unto death, sat in a Montreal public stand in *his* own province on St. Jean Baptiste Day as louts hurled refuse and bottles at his prime minister and himself. He didn't shout "Stop it you fools." He didn't cower and flee. Instead, he kicked his wooden leg into position and simply stood up to face the barrage. It was a gesture. But then, the old man was a governor general of Canada and people cared about him and his office.

PAULINE VANIER

Pauline Vanier. Widow of the Rt. Honourable General Georges Vanier, the first French-Canadian Governor General (1959-1967). Former Chancellor of the University of Ottawa and Patron of the Vanier Institute of the Family. Now in her eighties, she lives an active retirement in Troisly-Breuil, France. One daughter and four sons. Roman Catholic.

L ooking out from the upstairs bedroom window at *Les Marronnières*, you can just make her out in the morning mist. She has been in her garden for about 10 minutes, scissors in hand, to gather a small bouquet for the breakfast table. The great swath of snow-white hair is quite lost in the mist and so the face — that great and warm and mothering face — seems especially etched with all the triumphs and ordeals of her times. She is a mere 83 in this memory from northern France where she still makes her retirement with an energy and passion that would lay low a person half her age — that lays herself low from time to time.

"I thought I was really and finally going gaga this winter," she announced when I arrived for this particular visit. "I had a complete nervous breakdown. Weeping like a child. You never saw such a fool, such a nuisance . . ."

"Don't be absurd," I said, "you're far too old to have a nervous breakdown. It must have been something you ate."

She made the pretense of boxing me around my ears, but she laughed and her laughter is still more warming than a blazing hearth in mid-winter.

* * *

The first sight of her I ever had, curiously, was the most fleeting and enduring. She was in her appointed role as consort to General Vanier, who was then just beginning a long term as Governor General. I was in a dangerously defiant mood at the annual Prize Day ceremony in the Prayer Hall at Upper Canada College. My own prize, for winning the public-speaking competition the year before, was somewhat tainted in that I had left the noble establishment six months earlier under something of a cloud. This cloud was festooned with school-boy statistics and it was black and menacing: Physics — 12 per cent; Latin Authors — 42 per cent; Algebra — 38 per cent. The proverbial bad penny had turned up, inappropriately, on the very day when the college was honouring its best and brightest. Still, I'd won the prize and even if I wasn't at the school any more, I was damn well coming for my due. Fifteen is a great age to discover the universe is malevolent.

General Vanier lurched across the Prayer Hall stage, willing his artificial leg to do its work when it was perfectly clear — even then — that his body had tired of the struggle all those many years since the First World War. How fine he looked! Everyone who remembers him today still says that. The long ascetic face set off eyes that seemed to encompass infinite sadness until he smiled, when a small but indisputable twinkle of mischief overtook the vice-regal countenance. Since he was the Governor General, and we were impressionable school boys, we saw nothing else at first: not the old fraud who was Principal, not the masters, not the self-important prefects; not even his wife.

After the prizes for scholastic achievement were handed out, it came time to acknowledge the lesser endeavours. I remember climbing the stairs to the stage dais as the General perused the book he was about to give me. It was Rudyard Kipling's *Stalky and Company,* done up smartly in leather binding with the school's crest stamped in gold on the front.

"A good book," he said as he handed it to me, "but I expect you are a little old for it now. These things happen. At least you'll have one book in your library you can judge from its cover."

I didn't understand the joke, and the mood of defiance that I had taken right up to his presence had quite vanished and had been replaced by awe. Suddenly, as he was talking, I became aware of her. I looked to the right and saw that handsome, patrician face smiling with affection — at me, I vainly imagined, and only later realized that after all the decades of marriage she was still enthralled by his dry wit. Love was the well-spring of her actions and her moods then; today, the memory of that love haunts her home and governs a not altogether passive acceptance of growing old.

* * *

In the summer of June, 1966, Governor General and Mme. Vanier made their last vice-regal visit to Newfoundland. The senior reporter of the St. John's *Evening Telegram* called in sick the day after it began. In fact, the only thing seriously affecting his health was the thought of two more days of watching girl guides curtseying and provincial cabinet ministers posturing to the Vaniers. So this summertime reporter got sent to the Lodge in Bowater Park to report on the civic reception, already in full swing when I arrived.

By this time, he was older than old and clearly exhausted — not just from the round of duties he faithfully performed, but from life itself. As the mayor of St. John's and his tribe of councillors clustered around him, he tried gamely to keep up the patter of small talk. I can remember him saying: "Now don't destroy that harbour. It's a beautiful harbour." The politicians all concurred. It really *was* a beautiful harbour. Everyone from the mainland says the same thing. Are you enjoying your visit? What did you think of the plans for the South Hills development?

With the most serious of countenances, he tried to nod assent and interest to all the queries, and then clearly even the

18

nodding became oppressive. He began uttering half sentences that he let drift off into nothingness. I was watching him closely and in my imagination I felt he was a light year away: in battle maybe, or with de Gaulle; in paradise also, before his appointed time; perhaps simply in another community, any one of the hundreds he had loyally and uncomplainingly gone to, to hear variations of the same questions, the same problems.

"We've had such a good day, Mr. Mayor, how can we ever thank you?" She had moved right to where he was sitting. From recent practice, one assumed, she knew exactly when to take over. The General looked up at her with surpassing gratitude. She issued compliments with deft precision; feigned interest where none could surely have been; flattered outrageously; laughed obligingly at banal anecdotes. All the assembled worthies and Pooh Bahs glowed with self-satisfaction. And just as soon as she could, she got her old lover out of that place and safely resting. No one was the wiser.

"A great man, General Vanier. A real patriot," said the Chief Justice of Newfoundland to no one in particular (i.e., me) as he left the doorway of the park's lodge. As far as I had been able to observe, the Governor General had said nothing whatsoever to the Chief Justice. It was with Mme. Vanier that he had talked. The intertwining of souls had, at the very end of their long alliance, taken on a kind of physical manifestation.

Georges Vanier died a few months later and his widow had to travel far and wide to find some solace for her grief. Phlegmatic Canada assimilated its loss more quickly. Only during the quietest moments does the sense of longing for his valour and his constancy — for his faith in the country — make his absence seem so unbearable. Canadians have never really been able to erect the apparatus of veneration for the best among them. Modesty is part of the reason, and that becomes us; fear of measuring up and fear of cataloguing precisely how truly modest our vision is forms another part, and that is our shame and folly. Ironically, the sweet oblivion General Vanier's memory has embraced for most Canadians today would be exactly what he would have wanted. He believed in coping with the burden of the day and considered that the present — the only time when human beings can actually commit actions — was infinitely superior to the past, which wallowed in selective nostalgia, or the future, where so much grief was stored up for both the vain and the idealistic.

* * *

"Are you ready yet?"

The foghorn of a voice came barrelling up the stairs at *Les Marronnières*. Arthritis, depression, back pain, loneliness, colds, fear of senility: the charms of growing old, gracefully or not, are much touted by the young but rarely espoused by the practitioners.

We went on a walk through the miraculous Compiègne forest. It comes up almost to her back garden. Joining us are two of the young "assistants" at L'Arche, the home for mentally handicapped adults that her son, Jean, started here during the Sixties and which has grown to be a world-wide movement. If she had moved to this sombre setting to be closer to him, she soon realized it was a bit of vanity. He seems to be more away than present, but he has left her with not inconsiderable chores. She is unofficially in charge of mothering these serious young people whose job it is to nurse large bodies that often can't do anything for themselves. The "assistants" are wonderful people, in the thrall of an ecstasy of commitment that burns up their energies with awesome speed. Sometimes, in the game of outdoing each other in selflessness and service, there are casualties and *Les Marronnières* becomes a nursing station. Even among the sure-footed, a warm embrace from these ancient arms and a nice cup of tea form the very definition of survival.

As we all walk through the woods, she listens, just as she did with the councillors of the City of St. John's, and then gushes with compliments and encouragement. She knows her duty

20

and, mostly, does it, even admitting from time to time that listening to other people's problems and challenges helps to keep her own at bay. The disdain with which she holds her own contributions seems quite unaffected and is surely tied in to her natural fear *and* longing to meet the God it seems she has never really doubted. Vanities endure, of course. A journalist and friend, intent upon probing her memory, offers an occasional diversion which is not unacceptable.

It is not a life of a saint she leads, any more than it is some sort of model atonement delivered in gratitude for a full, rich and rewarding life. It is simply Pauline Vanier's life. The road to her French cottage was neither preordained or logical. If her son Jean's work is noble and a fitting tribute and product of her love for her husband, *Les Marronnières* in L'Arche is also just another place in the world to rest and prepare for the final adventure. Nevertheless, in this one place is both the ending and the beginning of a dream that is Canada's own, a dream in which "true patriot love" turns out to be faithfulness amidst doubt, modesty transforming pomp, and reconciliation to heal all the wounds.

BRIAN MULRONEY

Right Honourable M. Brian Mulroney, PC, MP, BA, LLL, LLD. Prime Minister of Canada. Born 20 March 1939 in Baie Comeau, Quebec. Educated at local schools, St. Francis Xavier University (Nova Scotia) and Laval University (Quebec). Called to the Quebec Bar in 1965, he joined the Montreal firm of Ogilvy, Cope, Porteous, Montgomery, Renault, Clark and Kirkpatrick and remained there as a partner until 1976. Appointed to the Cliche Royal Commission in 1974. Two years later he joined the Iron Ore Company of Canada where he served as executive vice-president for corporate affairs (1976-77) and president (1977-83). He was an unsuccessful candidate for the leadership of the Progressive Conservative Party in 1976, but got the nod eight years later. First elected to the House of Commons in 1983. Married, one daughter and four sons. Roman Catholic.

It is 1983, or thereabouts. I am bidden to John and Isabel Bassett's annual Grey Cup Brunch. Mulroney is there . . . not as tall, and far slurpier looking, than photos suggest. Big J hints that he has actually crashed the affair, riding on the coattails of ???? (ask M. Meighen who it was, or maybe it was Meighen himself.) Mulroney practically jitterbugs as he moves around all the tables, shaking hands and slapping backs. Poor form. He wisecracks a lot about Clark, which amuses everyone because he was on the tube three nights earlier pledging unyielding fealty and undying loyalty to poor Joe . . . . Going up near him for a closer look — this being the first time I have seen him in the flesh — I find that somehow my hand is outstretched. We shake. His palms are damp. Bad sign. Apparently President Nixon had damp palms too.

"I'm John Fraser of the *Globe and Mail*. I just wanted to say hello."

"J*O*H*N!!" he says, as if I were his long lost twin brother. He comes on far too strong for a first encounter. "Hey. You write terrific stuff. I was saying to Doyle (my boss) the other day, you just have to be the best damn journalist in the country."

Gee.

I find myself warming to him. The man's not subtle, of course, but Truth is always best when it is left unvarnished.

JAMES PETERSON

James Peterson. Former Member of Parliament, lawyer, businessman, extremely nice man. Brother of the Premier of Ontario, David Peterson. Married. Nicest trait: forgives journalists who use him unconscionably for devious purposes.

James Peterson entered and left the Canadian Parliament as a backbencher, although among friends an appointment to the cabinet of Prime Minister Trudeau was expected monthly. That it never came was more of a statement on the cabinet than on the kindest and most genial Member of Parliament of the past decade. Those who think of him as a lightweight, and there were quite a number in the Press Gallery and elsewhere who did, clearly never understood his gifts for reconciliation and pragmatic compromise. The Liberal Government could have used both.

When I first met him, during an extraordinary two weeks in 1974, he was still a rising tax lawyer and I was a dance critic. The twain would never have met except for the defection, in Toronto, of the Soviet ballet star Mikhail Baryshnikov. Before the first chapter of this tale was fully spun out, James Peterson would be weeping openly at the sight of a *tour en l'air* or an *entrechat dix*. But let me not get ahead of myself.

A small touring troupe of the Bolshoi Ballet was scheduled to make a Canadian visit before swooping down to Central America. The Soviet artistic authorities are terrible cheats and they understand the North American penchant for familiar labels. Practically anything that crawls artistically on a stage is labelled "Bolshoi" when it is exported for foreign consumption. The Bolshoi that came to Canada in the early summer of 1974 was an amazing ragtag collection of provincial second-raters and over-aged Establishment loyalists who had been thrown together in an unloving clump.

Two stars from Leningrad's mighty Kirov Ballet — Baryshnikov and ballerina Irina Kolpakova — had been tossed into the works to provide a bit of sheen. Among the ballet *cognoscenti,* the name Baryshnikov was even then an electric buzzword. A number of critics had seen him dancing either in Leningrad or during his one previous Western foray in London. Considered a trifle too short for a classic *danseur noble,* his athletic prowess, elegance and daring technical innovations nevertheless suggested he was the true heir to Nijinsky and Nureyev.

Consequently, despite the clowns he was surrounded by on stage, this tour had stirred up a remarkable degree of interest. A number of prominent New York ballet worthies actually left their redoubt in "the world's dance capital" and trekked up to Canada to see Baryshnikov dance, among them the New York *Times* dance critic Clive Barnes and his wife, Trish, who was a ballet enthusiast of occasionally alarming proportions.

I, of course, requested an interview with Baryshnikov but was rejected by the touring company's artistic director, a burly barrel of a former dancer named Alexander Lapauri. His wife, Raissa Strutchkova was actually billed as the leading ballerina but, in fact, this could only be true if top billing was based exclusively on brawn, shameless bravado, political machinations and sheer bullying.

Miss Strutchkova was no sylph. Heaven and her husband alone knew what she weighed on the scales. The sight of her in full battle dress — spiked *tutu,* fingers like stilettos set menacingly at the end of her pudding-dough arms and hands, garish smile painted on her face, and legs surely fashioned from the very heart of oak — would make the strongest of men tremble. Literally.

Her set piece for the ballet's O'Keefe Centre opening was the hideous *Walpurgis Night,* a bit of Soviet choreography that finally convinces you that there is no point in resisting the

Communist menace. The high point of this meat-grinder of a *divertissement* comes towards the end when the leading ballerina flings herself into the waiting arms of no less than three male dancers. Interpreted by Miss Strutchkova, *Walpurgis Night* is not so much a ballet about bacchanalia, as it is a re-enactment of the siege of Stalingrad. As she prepared to hurl herself in the air, her feet actually pawed the stage floor like a prize bull before the final charge on the matador. I looked closely at the three sacrificial males preparing to catch her and their knees were shaking. When she landed in their arms, the full impact sent them reeling back several steps and they looked like a mad vision of the cygnets in *Swan Lake* trying to carry a steel girder.

Returning to the newspaper to report on the carnage, I found the following message on my desk. "Trish Barnes from New York called and says it is extremely URGENT that you call her immediately." With my deadline less than an hour away, I was inclined to put the call off until afterwards but curiosity got the better of me and I was soon launched into a series of events that still make me shake my head in wonder. Mrs. Barnes turned out to be in full emotional flight.

"Do you speak Russian?" she demanded.

"Nyet."

"Well, maybe he speaks some French."

"Maybe who speaks some French?"

"Baryshnikov," said Mrs. Barnes. "You have to get a message through to him tonight or tomorrow. It's absolutely crucial. Clive and I tried to do it in Montreal, but the situation was impossible. Use all of your ingenuity and see what you can do. Have you got a pencil to take down a telephone number in New York?"

I got a pencil.

"Tell him his friends want to talk to him," said Mrs. Barnes, her voice becoming more and more similar to the Queen Mother's as she realized I was hooked. She probably got that idea because I kept saying "Yes, sir" to everything she demanded.

"What's up?" I asked. "Is he going to defect?"

"Now look. Don't ask questions. Just get to him. There's no question of defection. He has three very close friends here who simply have to make contact with him. Remember these names: Dina, Tina and Sascha. Got it? Dina, Tina and Sascha."

"Who are they?"

"Just remember the names. Dina, Tina and Sascha. And the phone number. Be very careful. There are some nasty people around him."

Just try writing a review in 30 minutes after that kind of a conversation.

Words somehow formed themselves as an over-active imagination worked in another sphere altogether and transformed a humble arts writer into the James Bond of ballet. When I read over the review before handing it to the editor, it was clear I was going to have to strike that night. After this review was read by Madame Strutchkova, there would be no opportunity for an encounter of any sort with anyone. A rhapsodic eulogy to Baryshnikov was used as a stick to beat his wretched cohorts on stage and I think there was even a line about the insult the *corps de ballet* represented to Soviet-Canadian relations.

My one chance was to nab Baryshnikov briefly at the Seagram's reception and it was there that I sped, faster even than Rudolph Nureyev escaping a fanatical female admirer. My preparations were all ready. I had written the New York phone number, complete with area code, on one side of a small sticky label. This was carefully fixed to the inside of a gold ring that I had switched from the left to right hand. My idea was that at the appropriate moment, I would shake hands with Baryshnikov and with the sticky side facing outwards, it would be affixed to his hand after we had unclasped. This bizarre idea came to me quite on the spur of the moment and was nearly the ruination of the whole effort.

By the time I arrived at the reception, the party was going full blast — or at least as full blast as a party comprised of people who don't understand each other's language could go.

There were about 30 large tables set up in the lower lounge, with the biggest in the centre for the Seagram's hosts and their special guests. These included Celia Franca, the founder and artistic director of the National Ballet of Canada, Madame Strutchkova, her hearty husband, several Soviet translators whom backstage gossip had it were all KGB guardians, and Baryshnikov.

It was my first sight of him close up, and he looked tired, bored and frustrated. Some impulsive inner demon which had taken over all my motor functions by this time, told me that I should effusively greet Miss Franca first, so that Baryshnikov would see that I was not some Canadian dupe of Soviet intelligence out to trap him. I admit my imagination was working overtime, but you never knew. Miss Franca and I had a kind of unspoken understanding. We liked each other, but since I wrote about her company more than anyone else in the country, I had to allow her periods when she could dismiss me as an ignorant lunatic of surpassing irrelevance. For her part, she had to make do with occasional shirty comments about "vulgar standards" and "dictatorial spite." Other than this, we had a warm relationship during those years.

She was surprised to see me, and to this day I am convinced that she instinctively knew what I was up to, for she played her role to the hilt. Those who have seen the great lady perform Madame Capulet in *Romeo and Juliet* or Madge in *La Sylphide* know well the parameters of the hilt.

"You must meet Mischa!" she said, pointing me in Baryshnikov's direction. Now I hadn't planned for this quite yet. Everyone at the table was watching us and nothing could be passed to anyone at this juncture. I mumbled a *"bonjour"* to him and got a mumbled *"bonjour"* back. At this point, the catering company official had come over with his seating arrangement list and informed me that I could sit at table 20. There seemed to be a hint in his voice that I should buzz off from head table.

Table 20 turned out to be a bit of a downer, although there

28

was one couple I knew. This was Senator and Mrs. Jack Godfrey of Toronto. Senator Godfrey was a former president of the National Ballet and the father of Stephen Godfrey who, ironically enough, later became the *Globe's* dance critic. The rest of the table, as I remember it, was comprised of Soviet artists, none of whom could speak a word of English. Since the Godfreys' Russian was as good as mine, there was a hell of a lot of mime. The ever-game Mary Godfrey managed to establish that one of our table companions was the ballet orchestra's conductor, and, being the lady she is, tried to find out his interests. "Fishing? Do you like fishing?" said Mrs. Godfrey as she mimed the art of the compleat angler.

"Da! Da!" shouted the conductor. "Fishing. Fishing." He too cast out a metaphorical line into the turbulent waters of the O'Keefe and it was precisely at this juncture that inspiration returned.

"We need a translator," I announced firmly. "This is ridiculous."

I marched authoritatively to the head table. On Baryshnikov's right hand side was the surly translator who had assisted me in the interview with Madame Strutchkova. She and her husband had, by this time, gotten up from their seats and were talking to colleagues at a neighbouring table.

I put both hands firmly on the shoulders of the translator and had the satisfaction of feeling him flinch wildly from the embrace.

"You are needed at Table 20," I said. "There's a Canadian senator there having a terrible time communicating with the conductor and all sorts of misunderstandings are going on. There are few people more important in my country than a Canadian senator and you must help him immediately."

The translator was disinclined to go, but his nominal boss —Mr. Lapauri, the artistic director —had come over to see what I was bellowing about. Some Russian words were exchanged and the upshot was that the translator headed towards Table 20. One down, one to go. On the other side of

Baryshnikov was a Soviet female official of unknown (to me) status. In any event she didn't look friendly. Just as I was wondering what to do about her, Miss Franca approached and I simply grabbed Baryshnikov's arm, pulled him up and said "we three must talk." Memory fails me on specifics at this point, but at some juncture during the next four or five minutes I got him alone. His French turned out to be worse than mine, so we understood each other perfectly. I said the magic three words — Dina, Tina and Sascha — and his whole face lit up in the most wonderful amazement.

"Ici? Maintenant?" he demanded.

"Non, non. À New York. J'ai ici le numéro du téléphone." I coyly turned my palm up. To my horror, the little strip of sticky paper had curled all up and was glued to the ring itself. The palm itself was awash in nervous sweat. Fortunately, it peeled off and the figures were still distinct. Baryshnikov laughed out loud, reached into his pocket and pulled out a notebook.

"Avez-vous un stylo?" he asked.

Hmmm. Hahaha. Hmmm.

"Non."

A journalist without a pen. Right. PANIC. I turned to the first person at the smaller table we were standing beside. "Have you got a pen, a pen or pencil?"

No. But his neighbour did. And then I read out the telephone number to Baryshnikov from my tiny piece of sodden sticky paper and, just as I was returning the pen to its owner, both Miss Franca and Mr. Lapauri approached us. He said something to Baryshnikov in Russian which made the dancer snort cynically and blurt out what I took to be rude swearwords. Some time later, I learned that Lapauri had sarcastically asked Baryshnikov "how much Franca offered you to join her company?" to which Mischa had replied: "Half a million, but I'm holding out for more."

* * *

Five days later he defected and was hidden away — complete with Dina, Tina and Sascha — in a country house north of Toronto. I had only suspected Baryshnikov would make the jump and didn't know when he would do it. With unprecedentedly adroit timing, I flew to Newfoundland for a holiday at the precise moment Jim Peterson, Mischa's new-found lawyer, spirited him away from the O'Keefe Centre following the final Toronto performance. Through sheer coincidence, the country house Baryshnikov was taken to was owned by mutual friends of Peterson and myself. When I got a phone call in St. John's telling all, I was — how shall I put it? — somewhat pained. Still, I wrote the first story on the defection from Newfoundland and since this was the only account of what actually happened and the dancer himself remained decisively hidden away, I became the focus of a certain measure of journalistic curiosity. Being in Newfoundland for three days added a rather amusing mystery to the piece, since no one could figure out how it fit into anything.

Upon my return, it was agreed that I would go up to the farm and start work on the first extensive and unfettered interview Mikhail Baryshnikov would give in the West. Peterson, who I had not yet actually met, was in a state of high jitters. His task was to organize the appropriate papers for Baryshnikov and to keep his whereabouts secret until everyone was confident his position was secure. When I phoned him at the farm, you would have thought I was talking to the CIA's chief spy inside the Politburo.

"We don't know who might be observing us," he said, immediately making me nervous. "That's a small rural exchange we are talking through. Anyone could be listening in."

Clearly, I thought, this is a man with a mission.

Turning back to the fray, I set about the task of figuring out who Dina, Tina and Sascha were. It seemed straightforward enough. Dina was Dina Makarova, a freelance photographer with ties to the American Ballet Theatre in New York. She spoke Russian and interpreted for Baryshnikov. Sascha was

Alexandre Minz, a former character dancer with the Kirov Ballet and a friend of Baryshnikov's. As a Jew, he had been allowed to immigrate a few years earlier and had ended up, as most good dancers do, in New York. And then there was Tina, or Christina Berlin. The daughter of a Hearst newspaper executive, she was a full-blown ballet groupie who had fallen in love with Mischa during fleeting encounters in the Soviet Union after they first met in London during a 1970 Kirov tour. She was beautiful and emotionally fragile.

By the time I had actually arrived on the scene, the trio was beginning to show some signs of being cooped up together for too long. Tina was madly in love with Mischa and had already announced to anyone who cared to listen that "we are, in effect, married." Mischa wasn't so sure and the more she insisted, the less sure he became. A difficult business that got a lot more difficult in the days ahead.

It was also not the greatest time to find out who Mikhail Baryshnikov was. He had all the glamour of a superstar and some of the spoilt nature that comes in the baggage. Yet there was also considerable evidence of boyish enthusiasm and fun. He brooded, certainly — what are Russians for if not brooding? —but he also hungered after rather mundane stability in social relations, at least with most of us. Obviously angered by the Soviet restrictions on his artistic ambitions, this was the only possible way in which one could see him as a victim of that system. For the rest, he was spoiled rotten: a vast apartment in a former palace, staff, his own car; in general as good a lifestyle as can be had behind the Iron Curtain. His brilliance as a dancer was established before he defected, so the Soviets cannot be accused of hampering him unduly. And yet he defected, causing embarrassment to the régime and, no doubt, hardships for colleagues and friends he left behind.

All this he forthrightly acknowledged as we talked throughout our first proper meeting. Dina tried gamely to keep up with the flow of words that came out, but from time to time had to scream, "STOP! I need a break and some tea." The only time I saw him come close to breaking down emotionally during this time was when we discussed what had gone on in his mind during the period he was trying to decide what to do. All he had wanted, he said, and his eyes were full of tears, was to have the chance of working with Western troupes. Every outstanding artist in the Soviet Union lusts for the same thing. "We don't want to leave. We don't want to cut our ties. But they force us and leave no alternatives."

On and on it went. When it came time to write the story, it was a difficult task trying to get as much human detail in without arousing the trepidation of a nervous committee of advisers. Everyone was a bit strung out. Early in the morning, I drove back to Toronto and to the apartment I had not seen since I left for Newfoundland. I was unamused to discover that it had been broken into and my papers ransacked. Next day, I learned that friends from Vancouver to St. John's (and throughout Toronto) had been telephoned by journalists from a competitor newspaper. I was advised to notify the police, but nothing was stolen and since I had left the front door key underneath the outside mat, I figured I would look like a fool, and did nothing.

Once the interview was published, exactly one week after the defection, life became more normal. Mischa moved back to the city, Tina was gotten rid of (the first of many women to discover Baryshnikov craved domestic bliss but not with any one woman for very long — a contradiction which still exists), and the way was prepared for his triumphant post-defection debut with the American Ballet Theatre in New York.

By this time, Peterson and I had become pals. His *bonhomie* was infectious and his charm considerable. He had bold connections with the Liberal Party and, before Baryshnikov travelled south, Jim arranged a fishing trip in Newfoundland of all places with no less than Liberal fixer Jim Coutts and Newfoundland Liberal leader Ed Roberts. Those of my *chers collègues* still pursuing the Newfoundland connection were utterly mystified and in the days to come I heard all sorts of theories delivered as gospel. From this I learned how coincidence and conspiracy form a natural alliance, against which mere truth hasn't a single hope.

"We're all going down for Mischa's debut," said Jim a few weeks later. "It's going to be an absolute gas."

Gas wasn't quite the word for it. Like rubes from outer Saskatchewan, our little band went down to the Big Apple and gawked from morning to morning. I can't for the life of me even remember what Mischa was dancing that night, but I remember Peterson jumping and and shouting "bravissimo" every time our hero blinked an eyelash. Balletomania had taken hold of the future Member of Parliament for Willowdale, vamped him and left him shouting more embarrassingly than a stage mother.

The party afterwards was memorable. Arriving at the Park Lane penthouse early, I walked into the living room to find Jacqueline Kennedy Onassis and her daughter Caroline. Just like that. Sitting in chairs. Drinking like real human beings. They were talking to someone who turned out to be Robert Massie, the author of *Peter The Great*. They looked up expectantly to see if I was Baryshnikov. I wasn't. And I heard a voice that certainly seemed to come from my own larynx actually say to Mrs. Kennedy:

"Hi. I'm John Fraser from Toronto. Haven't I seen you somewhere before?"

What causes such unwilling things to be said? I died a little, then and there. The lady herself simply said: "It's entirely possible."

"Even probable," said Mr. Massie with a snort.

Fortunately, they left soon after the star attraction turned up and took with them the memory of the *gaucherie*. I told Peterson what I had done and he immediately said: "Where is she? I'm going to ask her for a dance."

"She's gone, Jim," I said.

"You silly ass. Why didn't you ask her for a dance?"

"They weren't playing our tune."

In fact, they weren't playing anyone's tune. Peterson by this time was close to being uncontrollable, and his wonderful wife, Heather, clearly didn't give a damn. We were all as high as kites and no one had yet drunk a drop.

"Fraser, you've got to start playing that piano. I'm going to ask Makarova to dance," said Peterson. All amateur pianists require at least three people to insist they play before they will actually do the one thing they have been itching to do all evening.

I played the famous Scott Joplin rag that had been the theme song of *The Sting*. Peterson approached Natalia Makarova, only the most famous ballerina in New York, and asked her to dance. I just shook my head in disbelief. Imagine R.B. Bennett dancing with Pavlova. A woman came up to the piano and sat down on the bench beside me. "Keep going," she said, "it sounds nice."

Here was another familiar face. Where have I seen her before? A man looking alarmingly like Paul Newman approached us and whispered something in her ear. Sweet blessed Jesus, this is Joanne Woodward sitting beside me. I miss two chords, people notice. I am sweating. How the hell do I get out of this teenybopper's fantasy?

Sometime after midnight, the pumpkin arrived to take us all back to our hotels and thence to Canada where we have been, in one form or another, ever since.

* * *

From time to time, we all foregather and everything seems even sillier now than it did then. The last time was to celebrate the 10th anniversary of Mischa's unexpected arrival in our midst. The star himself was in great form and even danced with my four-year-old daughter who was sweetly oblivious to the momentous opportunity she had. Jim was the host. I made the speech. Mischa just laughed and shrugged his shoulders. He wanted us all to see the pictures of his three-year-old daughter whose mother, an American actress, he had split up with shortly after the birth.

"Maybe I have a lousy reputation with women," he said, "but look at these — you can see I know how to make a beautiful girl."

"Bravo Mischa," said Jim, "now what are you going to do for an encore?"

WILLIAM DAVIS

Honourable William Davis, PC, QC, MA. Bon vivant, wit and Special Envoy on Acid Rain. Former Premier of Ontario. Born 30 July 1929 in Brampton, Ontario. Educated at Brampton High School, University of Toronto and Osgoode Hall Law School. Called to the Ontario Bar in 1955 and first elected to the Ontario legislature in 1959. Minister of Education in Ontario from 1962-71 and Minister of University Affairs from 1964-71. Premier from 1971-85. The American Transit Association's "Man of the Year" for 1973. Married, with two sons and three daughters. United Church and a Freemason.

"Dear John," the letter began appropriately enough. "Congratulations on winning the National Newspaper Award for your thoughtful and incisive articles and critiques on the dance. This wonderful art form, which is finding new and wider audiences all the time, seems to express so many of our inchoate aspirations in ways even the spoken word has not proved adequate. The quality of your writing and the degree of refreshing enthusiasm you have always displayed is in no small measure directly related to the upsurge in interest one sees everywhere.

"Once again, my heartiest congratulations and good luck."

It was signed by the Premier of Ontario and I couldn't fail to see the logic of it all. How I had underrated this man in the past! How could I have possibly dismissed him as a mere remittance dispenser from Brampton? He and his charming wife, Cathy, were clearly artistic. This generous, although apt, letter was the sign of a sensitivity about which the public seemed wholly ignorant. I would correct that in the days to come. If a Medici prince was running the Province of Opportunity, he was damn well going to get his due.

It was with understandable excitement, therefore, that I learned this Diaghilev of politics was chosen to be the one to hand out the newspaper awards. On the evening of the big event at the Royal York Hotel, the award winners were invited to a pre-dinner reception where the Premier would have a chance to meet us informally.

"And what did you win an award for?" he asked when we were introduced. Scoff not at the question. A busy leader of a mighty people cannot be expected to remember every detail of his hefty correspondence.

"For ballet criticism, Sir," I said, waiting for the mask of incomprehension to fall and reveal a visage of high approbation.

"Ballet?" he said. His eyes narrowed and he took a couple of steps back. Nervously scanning the room, he shouted: "Cathy! Cathy! Over here!"

She approached, and he started to turn away, but not before he had pushed his wife in front of me. "She's the one in the family who knows all about ballet."

"I don't know anything about ballet. What are you talking about?" she said, shouting after him. But he was gone.

Perhaps if I had discussed the devastating effect of acid rain on *Swan Lake*, he might have lingered longer.

NORMAN ENDICOTT

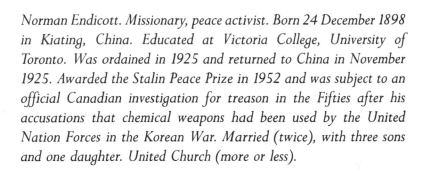

Norman Endicott. Missionary, peace activist. Born 24 December 1898 in Kiating, China. Educated at Victoria College, University of Toronto. Was ordained in 1925 and returned to China in November 1925. Awarded the Stalin Peace Prize in 1952 and was subject to an official Canadian investigation for treason in the Fifties after his accusations that chemical weapons had been used by the United Nation Forces in the Korean War. Married (twice), with three sons and one daughter. United Church (more or less).

You could tell he was a disputatious old bugger a mile off. It was the stubborn and deliberate way he walked and held his head, even though age had given him a bit of a stooped back and slowed the gait. Why I had agreed to meet him, I don't know. It was surely going to be a disaster. A West Indian physician living in Oshawa who had read my book on China as well as Dr. Endicott's biography thought it would be "interesting" to put us together. Interesting my eye, I thought as I approached the good doctor's front door. As interesting as putting a viper in the same cage as a mouse. Courage Fraser! Think mongoose. Stand your ground.

The ground to be stood was ideological. I had come away from China convinced that Chairman Mao Dzedong and what he had wrought were among of the definitive nightmares of the twentieth century, if not of all time. Dr. Endicott left China convinced that the Great Helmsman had presided over some oriental version of *Paradise Regained*. There was distance between us. When I read the final chapters of Stephen Endicott's book about his father, I spent most of my time quietly shaking my head and saying out loud the first line of a vaguely remembered Donne sonnet: "Busy old fool, why dost thou thus?" We had here, it seemed, a naive dupe of Communist propaganda; a man blinded by his own precepts; a victim of premature senility. The sort of person one loves to set up in savage recitatives like: "What the Norman Endicotts of this world utterly fail to comprehend is . . ."

How then can one explain that when I finally grasped his hand in introduction and we both broke out into wide grins, I knew I had embraced a kindred soul. It can, of course, be dismissed as the not unknown commodity of mutual absurdity, but pride and self-esteem force me to find other explanations. I knew the moment I laid eyes on him that we were brothers, that where he had been I somehow had been too, and what I had experienced in China — years later — was something I didn't in any way have to explain to him because it was known and felt and fully assimilated.

I don't dismiss the element of madness in all this. Clearly we both went out to China with fragments of Christian orthodoxy rattling around our brains. Also, as it does to all people who actually make it there, China had mysteriously altered the chemical juices that make up our perception. He came before Mao assumed titanic power; I came just after the overbearing old fraud had joined the mythical Yellow Emperor in the jade-encrusted afterworld reserved exclusively for Chinese despots, where everlasting vanity thwarts all the noblest aspirations of the heart.

Initially, the old man was as cautious as I was. This mood lasted for about 90 seconds. Dr. Endicott and I share the character traits of imprudence and provocativeness. We signed each other's tomes with sentiments a knight's move away from the truth. Our host bade us eat and we were placed beside each other at a large round table, the centrepiece of which was an electrically-operated lazy susan which went round and round, much like our bantering.

"You don't have enough history, that's the only problem," the old man said to me at one point. "I don't doubt your commitment to the Chinese people. I understand it perfectly. I admire it. But you don't know what it was like. The corruption. The destitution. The drug addiction. It was awful and stirred you to the quick. Mao offered the only hope, the only way out.''

I knew all this. I had been with him after all. The cartloads of dead in Shanghai. The fatuous unconcern of so many outsiders and their implicit racism in the contempt they held for the Chinese condition. The profiteering from misery. The young faces straining to hitch idealism to the presiding chaos, an exercise which hurtled them either into cynical opportunism or revolution. I raged at it all through him. Of course it was unacceptable. The God of Rosedale United Church had not passed by these scenes. He had merely clipped His coupons and sent a modest percentage to the appropriate missionary service to keep it all away from home. Lear went mad on the heath not because he lost his senses, but because he was too much in touch with them, because he saw what he hadn't seen before, knew what he hadn't understood before, felt what hadn't touched him before. Our God is a righteous God and if He seems to stand aloof from the fray, He has nevertheless given us the means to intervene, to make a difference. A quarter of the world's population have borne the evils of Western cupidity and imperialism and rapacious greed for long enough. Out with the sinners! Clean the temple from the humble back door to the high altar itself. Long live the revolution! Long live the great and long suffering and glorious Chinese people! God bless them! Mao save them!

That's me shouting Dr. Endicott. I do know my history and I have been embraced by the love and friendship of Chinese people. We share the same outrageous conceit: that even in exile we are among them and whether they care or not, their triumphs make us swell with pride and their tears fall down our own cheeks.

I didn't tell him this, of course, even though I felt it at the time. What I said to him was this:

"With all due respect, Sir, have you ever thought that perhaps you have too much history? Most of the Chinese who were my friends, like most of the Chinese people everywhere

41

today, have no direct knowledge of life before Mao. What you talk about is something bashed into their heads from a grotesque file labelled Lessons From History. And it comes to them terribly distorted and manipulated. It keeps being thrust on them in wave after wave of hysterical propaganda that they have either turned off entirely or have come to actively disbelieve. The corruption they have had practical experience with comes from Communist Party cadres. The capriciousness of leadership resides with the Politburo generally and the Great Helmsman specifically. The public executions, the lying, the knocks on the door at night, the arbitrary exercise of power, the ruthless factional fighting, the dead bodies on the street — these things they have seen are not the product of Chiang Kaishek and the hideous old Guomindang Party. It is their experience under Mao."

"You still need a context," he said. "You're not putting any of this against the Chinese experience throughout the past century. You can never forget we are talking about a billion people and thousands of years of continuous history."

I snatched an eggroll as it came whizzing by.

"And you mustn't forget that even with the most perfect knowledge of history, it is still necessary to get through the day and carry the burden of what you yourself have experienced. The only time for action is the present."

"I know that," he said with mounting impatience.

Our kind host intervened. "I knew this would be an interesting encounter! Didn't I say that to both of you?"

Dr. Endicott loaned me a battered copy of the book his first wife had written about China decades ago. She's dead now and he's married again, but when he handed it to me I knew I was receiving a testament of sorts. I have been trying to return the book to him for over four years but I can't bear to be parted from it. He shared deep things with her and, even today, wives and husbands can still share deep things. An illogical conjunction of two different generations of marriage is part of the reason I don't seem able to give up that book yet. And it is also a reminder that although we are still left on our separate ideological islands, we can see each other clearly across the water, through wind and weather. What I see is a fine old man who laboured night and day to be a pilgrim, and a valiant one at that. Misdirected, of course, but that seems somehow irrelevant.

CELIA FRANCA

———⊶ ⊷———

BETTY OLIPHANT

———⊶ ⊷———

Celia Franca, OC. Founder of the National Ballet of Canada in 1951. Born 25 June 1921 in London, England. Educated at the Guildhall School of Music (London) and the Royal Academy of Dancing. Made her dancing debut in 1936 as a member of the corps de ballet *in an Anthony Tudor ballet presented at London's Mercury Theatre. Soloist with Ballet Rambert from 1936-38 and then lead dramatic dancer from 1938-39. Performed and taught with various companies in England, including Sadler's Wells Ballet, before coming to Canada in 1951. Artistic director of the National Ballet of Canada from 1951-74, where, for many years she was also a principal dancer and choreographer. Married.*

Betty Oliphant, OC. Founder, artistic director and ballet principal of the National Ballet School. Born 5 August 1918 in London, England. Educated at Queen's College School and St. Mary's College School, both in London. Trained by Tamara Karvasina and Laurent Novikoff, she worked in and around London's West End as a choreographer, teacher and school principal. Came to Canada in 1947 and established the Betty Oliphant School of Ballet. Ballet mistress of the National Ballet of Canada from 1951-62. Founded National Ballet School in 1959. Associate artistic director of the National Ballet from 1969-75. Divorced. Two daughters.

U ntil a short time ago, it would have amused neither of these great ladies to be joined in print after they had so effectively and efficiently separated in fact. The bitterness of their professional divorce had for some years been legendary in Canadian dance circles. Considering the nature of their personalities, the tempestuous years of their partnership, their divergent social origins and the venom which afflicted their penultimate altercation, it is not mere caprice that forces me to reverse the matrimonial injunction: those whom God hath pulled assunder, this poor fool shall try to join together.

They are both my valued and esteemed friends, although it is true there has never been a break in my friendship with Betty, while Celia and I exchanged rhetorical blows and went through a difficult period. Yet in my mind, they are hopelessly entwined and in the history of dance in our country they remain embraced and bound to each other in a mesh of achievement more sturdy than the one Vulcan once fashioned in his rage of jealousy. The National Ballet of Canada and the National Ballet School are both extraordinary and remarkable institutions. How could they be otherwise, for they were founded and sustained by extraordinary and remarkable women.

If I say that both these Toronto-based establishments measure up to the best in the world, which they do, we can safely dismiss the ensuing critical qualifications and brickbats. The company has never produced a world-shattering choreographer and so has missed out on what is generally considered one of the cornerstones of greatness. In fact, the importance of a consummate genius like George Balanchine or Frederick Ashton working directly with a company is not so much overstated as misinterpreted. The two leading Soviet troupes, the Bolshoi in Moscow and the Kirov in Leningrad, have featured the work of quite frightful choreographers for years, but remain at the top of the list of "great" companies — thanks primarily to outstanding dancers, the best of whom generally defect to the West. The Royal Ballet of Great Britain is always considered right at the very top, but in fact as I am writing, it is in the second year of quite impressive decline. Even if that decline continues apace, the company will remain at the top of the list because of its historical reputation and because its home base is London and thus accrues, despite itself, the natural excitement that the great metropolis engenders simply by being London. Even the New York City Ballet, with its previous heritage of Balanchine ballets, is without the great choreographer himself, with no equivalent successor in sight.

Toronto is not New York or London and the National Ballet Company will always be up against the chauvinism of the self-defined national dance capitals of the world. Yet, in the end, this is piffle. The company — its repertoire, its dancers, its system — has been front-rank for several years. People confuse its venue with its calibre. In dance the whole world of value judgements is so ridiculously subjective and factional that there isn't even a hope of getting Canadians to accept the full panoply of hard-won excellence their premier classical ballet company represents.

As for the National Ballet School, it has offered the best classical training available anywhere for many years, a fact acknowledged in rueful (private) conversation even by Lincoln Kirstein, who, with Balanchine, made the New York City Ballet what it is. If Lincoln had had his way, he would have packed the entire establishment up and moved it to Lincoln Centre ages ago. Instead, like the directors of so many European and North American ballet academies, he has been forced to come to Toronto, make notes and try to emulate.

None of this was achieved, however, without some cost. By focusing on the two ladies most directly responsible, one does not diminish either their successors or subordinates, the women's committees or the volunteer fund-raisers, the Canada Council or the teachers. Nor is one trying to cover up any of the less inviting traits of the Misses Franca and Oliphant: the rebels and failures of the school and company are sometimes as eloquent on the deficiencies of the National "system" as the Karen Kains and Frank Augustyns are on its undoubted successes.

In the end, though, the school and the company are so thoroughly the creatures of Betty and Celia that any attempt to get around this singular fact is doomed to irrelevancy.

I began a happy and exciting career as a dance critic for the *Globe and Mail* at a time in the early Seventies when both the company and the school were well launched into the big-time. It was also the last period of discernible public peace between the two *grandes dames* until very recently. By the time I was appointed to succeed Herbert Whittaker as drama critic of the paper, Betty and Celia could barely mention each other's name without spitting it out. From time to time, the dispute — which seemed to me to be composed of equal measures of hurt and mutual misunderstanding — would flare up in public in particularly dramatic ways. Betty has always been the better politician and far more astute tactician. When Celia, after announcing her retirement, tried to arrange affairs at the National Ballet Company through a hand-picked successor who would allow her a continuing and important behind-the-scenes role, Betty set about to scuttle the idea with a battle plan that von Clausewitz would have doffed his hat to. Although the company and the school are officially separate institutions, the overwhelming preponderance of school graduates in the National corps assured Betty of troops in the trenches, while her own consummate skills of persuasion and debt-collection gave her instant access to the company's board, the media and fund raisers. To this day, I'm not entirely convinced Celia understands the full panoply of power that was deployed against her carefully wrought plans. David Haber, her successor, had a much shorter stay in office than John Napier Turner.

Celia had her revenge, however. After the dust and chicken feathers had all settled, the company held a grand gala in her honour at the O'Keefe Centre. At the conclusion of the evening, during which her pre-eminent role as the founder of the company had been served up with noisy hosannahs and loud alleluias, she delivered a long speech in which she singled out dozens of people for special praise. It was a devilishly wicked speech, because she built it up with consummate craft on a hierarchical scale of importance. Those in the know knew exactly what she was up to. The name of each honoured contributor to the company's development was preceded by a kind of guessing game as she praised the particular talents and genius of the person yet to be identified.

Betty sat in the audience, metaphorically on the edge of the seat. Unless one was aware of her insecurities, her desire (like all great artists) to be recognized, her longing to be appreciated, her unrelenting struggle for co-equal status with Celia, one could not fully appreciate what the Founder on the stage was up to. As each accolade was spun out, it seemed as if Celia was going to draw a line between her private quarrel with Betty, and give her her due. And each time, it turned out to be someone else. Like the dance of the cats in *The Sleeping Beauty,* she repeated the steps and mime again and again. Celia brought her nemesis to the verge of accolade a half dozen times and then sent her crashing back into anonymity on each occasion.

My editor, Richard Doyle, was in the audience and he saw the last act of this particular revenger's drama. Betty was borne out of the amphitheatre of O'Keefe Centre supported by two men holding either arm. She was in tears and close to fainting. The perpetual pain in her back had, on this notable occasion, given way to the deep wounds in her heart and to her self-esteem. The score was 30-all, but on this night it was not clear who had the next service.

These events could be deplored or enjoyed, depending on your vantage point. At the time, my partisanship was rather exclusively directed towards Betty and I took this incident as yet another tacky example of Celia's well-known vulgarity. When she retired, Celia and I had not parted company well. As I remember our last conversation on the telephone, concerning a review I had written, the receiver had fairly melted in my hand. The dear lady had a way with words and I recall something to the effect of: "When you didn't know anything about ballet, you were quite an interesting writer on the subject; now that you've learned a tiny bit, we all think you've become a monumental bore." I believe I parried with something equally graceful, but before I concluded she had slammed down the phone.

In time, I came to see that the wonder of it all was not this or that atrocity the two could perpetrate on each other, but rather that they had formed such a dynamic and successful partnership for so long. The company and school did get founded and both of them went through terrifically hard times. It is forgotten now, but ballet dancers used to have to go on the dole (unemployment insurance compensation, to be more precise) at the end of each unappreciated season in order simply to survive. Not only did these two ladies have to create institutions, they had to endure years of disinterested sniggering as they sought to build up the basic appreciation necessary for their creations to truly survive beyond their pioneering work. I suspect that Celia never understood, perhaps does not to this day, Betty's craving to be at centre stage even while she kept firmly behind the scenes. On the other hand, Celia had a natural gift of invention and a certain kind of creativity that was deployed so effortlessly and grandly, that Betty probably never fully understood the forces of competitiveness and jealously which they aroused in her. Like a Christian Scientist and a medical doctor I know who were married for two decades and had three children, the wonder was not that they split up eventually, but that they had stayed together for so long and had produced such estimable offspring.

Looked at on their own, the two ladies remain among the most remarkable citizens in the land. If it is true Betty is no constitutional monarch at the National Ballet School and, from time to time, there have been waves of subterranean rebellion at the authority she wields so effortlessly, it is also true that she is simply a wonder when she is in her element. Through astute recruiting choices, she has transformed the image of the male dancer in Canada, and the way she can zero in on genuine star material and push young dancers to the extremities of their talent and potential is a gift every bit as valuable and crucial as a choreographic triumph, even if it doesn't register in such obvious ways. Like all geniuses who are also activists in their chosen endeavours, Betty remains a source of controversy and quite appalling jealousies. From time to time, her motivations have been scrutinized with microscopic intensity. That she has erred with her tactics and troop deployments from time to time is obvious, but her motivation, which is something quite apart from any personal grievances she may maintain, is the purest and noblest thing about her. It is a drive towards excellence in an art that has had to fight its way for respect into the Canadian consciousness. Betty is incapable of compromise on basics. Anyone who thinks otherwise doesn't understand her at all. If she has made a bad judgement she is as ruthless on herself as on anyone else; and there are very few people in the entire world of the performing arts who understand more perfectly the creative and motivating force in the critical impulse.

It would take me longer to discover what I felt made Celia tick and the fact that I now think I know what it is, I owe to the quirks of fate. When I was posted to Peking as my newspaper's eighth China correspondent, some people — and I certainly do not hold it against them, as the identical thought struck me from time to time — felt it was a trifle bizarre to send a ballet critic to the land of the Mao Zedong. In time, I came to see that my early training in ballet politics prepared me wonderfully well for dealing with the murderous factionalism of the Chinese Communist Party. "One always divides into two," the Great Helmsman had once opined, and when Mao's widow, Jiang Qing, let fly at the diminutive Deng Xiaoping in a cosmic series of recriminations, and he set about to trap and humble her, you will not be surprised to learn that I felt I had heard it all before.

In any event, I was not prepared for the news from the Canadian Embassy when the Cultural Affairs officer told me that Miss Celia Franca had been invited by the Chinese Ministry of the Arts to come to the People's Republic and assist in the professional rehabilitation of the country's leading ballet company after years of drift, decay and corruption thanks to the Cultural Revolution. For 12 bruising and killing years, the company had been permitted to perform only three full-length ballets and a half-dozen proletarian *divertissements*, the choreographic subtlety of which all revolved around the attack position of a guerilla soldier with an unsheathed bayonet.

In effect, Celia was being asked to begin a new company under infinitely more complicated conditions than she ever encountered in waspish Toronto during the early Fifties. At our first meeting, we both viewed ourselves in our new guises with uncharacteristic bashfulness and then she was pulled into the vortex of dozens of Chinese dancers' and teachers' fervent desire to draw every last ounce of her considerable energy.

And she gave it. Unstintingly. Before my eyes, I saw her strip away the years. She quite literally rolled up her sleeves and before the first day's session had ended she had issued specific orders to make changes in everything from the kind of ballet shoes the young women were wearing (and destroying their feet with) to the very philosophy of the opening, warm-up classes. The comprehensiveness of her gaze and concern were awesome, and the pragmatic way in which she seized anything positive she saw, and built up her more serious criticisms around this diplomatic and helpful base, revealed a Celia Franca I hardly knew existed. And she pushed herself harder than anyone else on the floor, so that there were times when she seemed to be physically willing them into the kind of effort and commitment that had been deployed in the monstrous political campaigns of the past, but never the art itself.

On that day, I saw — or so I believe — the determined and lonely young woman who turned up in Toronto all those years ago with only a vision to sustain her energy and drive. I saw what Betty saw, and will even admit in a quiet and unthreatened moment today: Celia is a force of nature which cannot be resisted. Unleashed in the appropriate setting, it is boundlessly exciting to observe.

The feud these great ladies had must be viewed in the context of their accomplishments. In that light, it is of no account whatsoever. A short time ago, sitting in a living room in England, they appeared together on a British Broadcasting Corporation documentary on the National Ballet Company and National Ballet School. A truce had clearly been declared and not just for the purposes of the television cameras. To watch them in the country they originally came from, fussing and clucking over the *Canadian* institutions they had created and were identified with, seemed to me as fine a *dénouement* as one every gets in this fractious world.

JOHN CROSBIE

―――――◁ ▷―――――

Honourable John Carnell Crosbie, PC, QC, BA, MP. Minister of Justice and former Minister of Finance. Born 30 January 1931 in St. John's, Newfoundland. Educated at Bishop Field College (Newfoundland), St. Andrew's College (Ontario), Queen's University, Dalhousie University and the University of London (England). Called to the Newfoundland Bar in 1957. His first foray into politics was wildly successful in 1965 when he ran for city council and toted up the most votes thereby automatically becoming Deputy Mayor. Within a few months, Premier Joseph Smallwood nabbed him for the provincial cabinet where he was appointed Minister of Municipal Affairs and Housing. He later became Minister of Health but in 1968 a terrible falling out with Mr. Smallwood resulting in his resignation from the cabinet and the provincial Liberal Party. For a short period he sat as an independent but then joined the Newfoundland Progressive Conservative Party. In 1972, under a new PC administration, he became Minister of Finance and President of the Treasury Board in Newfoundland. Other offices he served in locally, before entering federal politics in 1976, included: Minister of Fisheries, Minister of Inter-Governmental Affairs, Minister of Mines and Energy. In the short-lived administration of Prime Minister Joe Clark, he was Minister of Finance. An unsuccessful candidate for the leadership of the federal PC party in 1984, he now serves as Minister of Justice and Attorney General in the administration of Prime Minister Brian Mulroney. Married, with two sons and one daughter. United Church.

O n the eve of his short-lived government's defeat at the polls, the Minister of Finance was making wonderful, biting jokes. He knew he would be personally re-elected in his St. John's East riding, but that Joe Clark's little dream was all but played out. Like Mercutio with a fatal stab wound, John Crosbie wisecracked right to the bitter end.

It had been some years since I had stood in his second-floor study on Circular Road. From the windows you could see the grounds of Newfoundland's Government House, residence of the lieutenant governor. The view had been unchanged for over a century. Inside the study, however, there were changes. Didn't there used to be an awful seascape over the mantel? Maybe. Maybe not. The minister couldn't remember. In any event, there was no denying the central art work this day. It was a huge and lurid reproduction of Salvador Dali's crucifixion scene. Christ is on His cross, but he is set against a background that is the universe itself, with the planets and stars twinkling benignly away. On the rim of the planet Earth, a draped female figure looks at Him with stoic concern. I took her to be Mary Magdalene.

Knowing that Crosbie's riding was predominantly Roman Catholic and that he was from an old Methodist family, I asked rather sarcastically if the Dali was up there "to impress your parishioners."

"No, no," he said, standing back to savour the holy scene, "that's my beloved leader Joe Clark up on that cross."

"It is?" I said. "Then who is the female figure?"

"Ah," answered the Minister. "That's Maureen, who put him there."

Do these lines materialize from nowhere, filched from thin air? After the defeat, the anger inside Crosbie could scarcely be contained. He and his wife Jane decided to take a big trip to the People's Republic of China and blot the memory of the Tory party's political ineptitude — Joe's ineptitude — from his mind. I was consulted on an itinerary. Later, at the Chinese Embassy, when the former minister spoke to the obliging ambassador, he made the mistake of mentioning my name. An oblique harangue ensued and, wisely, my name was spoken no more. The night before he and Jane flew from Toronto to China, my wife and I had dinner with them. In the mellowness that came with wine and candlelight, I decided to be stinky and smoke him out:

"That was a curious statement you made to my newspaper this morning. What was it you said: 'Clark's position as leader of the Progressive Conservative Party was safe as a church'? Did you really say that?"

"Yes, my son, I said that."

I snorted ungenerously. I tried to convey in that snort that the hypocrisy of politicians knows no bounds. Crosbie's eyes narrowed:

"The trouble with you twits in the media is that now that I'm not a Minister of the Crown, you don't stick around for the end of my quotes."

"What was the end of your quote?" I asked, walking all unsuspecting yet again into his favourite sort of trap.

"Safe as a church in China."

* * *

Back, back, back. 1968 and '69. St. John's again. The provincial legislature. Joey Smallwood is at the zenith of his power and controls 39 of the 42 seats in the House. John is a minister here too, municipal affairs or something like that. Not two sentences come out succinctly. He stumbles and fumbles. The eyes roll up heavenwards, but his hands are shaking and the papers in them rattle like Lady Windermere's fan. On an island of gifted *raconteurs* and outrageous public speakers, he is Grief itself: the worst speaker in the legislature.

As for the legislature, it looks like a set for a comic opera. All the members' seats are moveable, and so the opposition side has only three lonely little desks. Even the legislature in Albania has a more equitable-looking appearance. Smallwood actually has a majority of the entire membership sitting in his cabinet, if you include the Speaker's position. Even if all his backbenchers defected, about as likely as Stalin's Politburo bolting the authority of the Little Father, Joey would still command the confidence of the House. Every Liberal halo comes with a perk or two.

What a great deal of history there has been between Joey and the Crosbies. John's father, Mr. Ches, employed the "scrappy guttersnipe" from time to time and financed some of his screwball schemes. Like the piggery in Gander during the war. Mr. Bill, John's uncle and Mr. Ches' younger brother, told me the story. Joey had a brilliant scheme to start a piggery in Gander to supply fresh pork to all the airmen stationed there. As the Chinese have known for several millenia, pigs are wonderful cash machines: they eat garbage and hardly an ounce of their bulk can't be sold and consumed.

The Gander piggery seemed to go well. The work was hard and if the profits weren't spectacular, they were nevertheless steady. It was a good little business. Nor was life uneventful. One day, calamity struck. Joey, for some time, had had an arrangement with the airbase to collect its garbage to provide swill for the pigs. This had nice cyclical symbolism tied to the food chain. Unfortunately, a new mess sergeant was appointed who hadn't been informed of the arrangement and was a stickler for the book. The book told him that his waste food products and garbage that were sent to the dump, where Smallwood's staff collected it, should be generously laced with lime to aid in decomposition. For several days this spicy concoction was fed to Joey's pigs and, not very surprisingly, they began to drop dead. It was a particularly gruesome death too, with the pigs shaking and squealing "something terrible."

According to Mr. Bill, Joey quickly sized up the extent of the crisis and made a quick decision: all the pigs had to be slaughtered. When this bloody deed was done, much of the meat was sold to the base and the piggery had to start almost from scratch again.

Mr. Ches and Joey came to a mighty parting of the ways during the great battle over Confederation. Crosbie thought Newfoundland should retain its independence but seek economic union with the United States, while Smallwood of course was busy selling the idea of becoming a province of

Canada. Nearly two decades later, the two sons of Mr. Ches — Andrew and John — were thick as thieves with the Smallwood administration: Andrew as one of the richest and most powerful tycoons on the island, and John as a cabinet minister. But something went terribly wrong. Taciturn and inexpressive as he was, John finally couldn't stomach life with Joey and decided to bolt, not just from the cabinet but the party itself, to sit as an independent (and later as a Tory).

That sort of thing just wasn't done in the Newfoundland of the Sixties. The Only Living Father of Confederation ran a tight ship. This is the same man, for example, who said he would send down a plane-load of character witnesses to assist the wicked financier, John C. Doyle, with his trial on stock fraud charges in the United States. The plane would carry, said Joey, the Chief Justice of Newfoundland, the Minister of Justice (and half the cabinet), the President of Memorial University of Newfoundland (who had bestowed an honorary degree on Doyle and named a residence after him for donations that were never received), men of the cloth and leading citizens from "every walk of life."

Smallwood unleashed a ferocious attack not only on the defecting Crosbie, but on the whole family. He was particularly successful in raising the spectre of Andrew Crosbie's dark business dealings with the government. Because people had always disliked the most flamboyant of the Crosbies and were sure anyone that rich must have been up to no good, the mud stuck. For John, it was rock bottom. If he had stammered a little before, he now became incomprensible, mumbling ineffective defences and leaving the general impression that Smallwood probably had a lot more on him and his perfidious clan. No one seemed to wonder why — if Andrew Crosbie was up to no good in securing government contracts and John was the linchpin inside the cabinet — Smallwood had condoned their behaviour so helplessly all these years. There was the smell of a political lynching in the air and the mob was aroused. The House of Crosbie seemed to be teetering.

Mr. Bill, a private businessman and my good and noble friend, watched the unfolding drama with a strange mixture of dread and satisfaction. The satisfaction came from the confirmation he was receiving that Joey was everything he had always thought him to be. As young John retreated increasingly into his incoherent shell, Joey became emboldened. On the third or fourth day of the crisis, he expanded the attack to include Mr. Bill, but this time he made his charges about influence-peddling outside the immunity of the House.

"Now we've got him," said Mr. Bill in triumph. I had dropped in on his house during the lunch-hour and found him in high spirits. "Just watch what happens now."

Lawyers were speedily summoned and stern letters delivered to the Premier's office. Whatever it was they contained, it worked like a charm. Later that evening, the Minister of Justice phoned Mr. Bill and I was in the room when the call came.

"We're trying to make it easy on the Skipper," the Minister reportedly said over the telephone.

"Look," said Mr. Bill, winking at me and putting on his sternest mien, "you tell that little bastard if he doesn't retract every single goddammed word and make a public apology, I'm suing."

Slam.

"That," he said, "should be easy enough for even the Skipper to understand."

Eight hours later, the retraction and the apology came and the festering boil was lanced. In the legislature, John made a clumsy effort to call a truce, which was accepted by the Premier. That day, in the St. John's *Daily News* — which his brother Andrew owned at the time — the banner headline read: JOHN CROSBIE THANKS PREMIER. John was livid with rage but later Mr. Bill said it was surprising the *Daily News* had even been able to get that much sense out of John's speech.

"Somehow," said Mr. Bill, "he's got to become quicker on his feet or he's going to go nowhere fast."

Between those days and the time when John Crosbie emerged as the master of Question Period quip, this self-conscious and agreeable man remade himself. It was partly done with the help of Dale Carnegie, but mostly it came from a determined effort to find himself, and have the courage to reveal it. Perhaps he would not have been a good prime minister, but he has immeasurably enlivened the political life of the nation and for this much praise is due.

NORTHROP FRYE

Northrop Frye, CC, DD, LLD, DLitt, Dde l'U, LHD, FRSC. University professor, author, critic. Born 14 July 1912 in Sherbrooke, Quebec. Educated at local schools in Sherbrooke, University of Toronto, Emmanuel College (Toronto), Merton College (Oxford). Ordained into the ministry of the United Church of Canada in 1936. A long career with Victoria College at the University of Toronto beginning in 1939 (lecturer, professor, Chairman of the English Department, principal and chancellor). Foremost living critic of English literature, a reputation built on numerous publications the most famous of which include: Fearful Symmetry *(1947),* Anatomy of Criticism *(1957) and* The Great Code *(1983). Innumerable prizes, awards and honorary degrees. Dislikes small talk. Married.*

A friend of mine (call him R) from Trent University was once assigned the task of driving Dr. Frye from Peterborough to Toronto after he (Frye) had delivered another of his seminal lectures on literature and life. R refreshed himself on some of the key themes which Dr. Frye had become so identified with over a lifetime of conspicuous scholarship. For days, R said, he quietly savoured the prospect of being alone with the great man and discussing some of the great critical issues of our times.

Lecture delivered and lecturer duly placed into the custody of R, Dr. Frye obediently took his position in the front passenger seat. One gathers R began *pianissimo*, leading up to a grand expostulation about a particular Frye theory which, R insisted, laid bare the whole structure of literature and for which he, R, would always be grateful.

Dr. Frye, who never once turned away from looking out the

side window, listened patiently to all this, and then replied in his well-known monotone, "You've got it all wrong. You haven't understood a thing."

For the rest of the trip, not one other word was spoken.

* * *

Some years after this incident, I had the chance to meet Dr. Frye at a small dinner party given by M at her large Forest Hill Village mansion. Primed by R's cautionary tale, I tried to avoid any baroque compliments. Thanks to this wise course of action, I discovered that the good professor has a higher tolerance for young journalists than young academics. I noticed a slight edge of sarcasm as he noted the number of honorary degrees Margaret Atwood had already chalked up, but was astute enough not to ask how many he himself had been given. Eventually, I worked up sufficient confidence to try out journalistic anecdotes, which were received with grace and kindness. Fully unleashed now, I quickly found myself entering forbidden territory and actually heard something inside me chattering on about archetypes and their pattern in newspaper stories. Such fits of compulsive blather are my curse. The more desperate I was to stop and find a corner to hide away in, the louder and sillier I heard my own voice becoming.

"Well, all I know is that you can't eat an archetype and this dinner is really good."

Bless her wonderful soul, it was Mrs. Frye to the rescue. She smiled across the table at me and said she had always thought a journalist must have a wonderful and interesting life. I dissolved in gratitude, totally agreed and never once touched on the subject of how silly the profession can encourage you to be at times.

At this dinner, which M presided over with her usual efficiency and attentive pride, there had been a debate about the state of elementary and high-school education in Ontario. M was not convinced that her only son was getting the stimulation and challenge she felt he was capable of responding to. In fact, he was bright enough and, perhaps as a form of self-protection, chose to be clever in exactly those areas M had no interest in. The real focus of this discussion was, in fact, below stairs watching television, a not unfamiliar activity for 13-year-olds. M suddenly decided a unique opportunity was at hand. Would Dr. Frye go downstairs to chat up the lad and see if there was anything stirring in that little brain of his?

With perfect politeness, the greatest living English-language literary critic descended to the "rec" room below and sat down to watch the end of *Kojak*. The scene had too much to savour for me to remain quietly upstairs with the rest. I asked for the directions to the washroom and at once snuck down to the basement. The scholar and the boy were both glued to the tube, which provided the only light in the gloomy room. After a particularly violent scene of fighting, Dr. Frye said:

"That was quite something, wasn't it?"

"I suppose so," said M's son. "He does it every week."

More silence as Telly Savalas played host to the two solitudes.

"I suppose you have some favourite books," said Dr. Frye.

"Which ones?" asked the boy.

"I don't know. I'm asking you."

"My science textbook is pretty good."

Silence.

"Well, I suppose I better be getting upstairs," said Dr. Frye.

"Bye," said the boy.

* * *

I duly reported all this to R, but I'm not sure it assuaged the remembered pain of the drive to Toronto.

BARBARA AMIEL

Barbara Amiel, CC, OM, PhD, DLitt. Former Editor and leading quidnunc *of the Toronto* Sun. *Born on a still undisclosed date in an undisclosed village in Hertfordshire, England. Educated at St. Paul's School (London), Exeter College (Oxford), Sorbonne (Paris), London School of Economics, Princeton University. Contributor to numerous leading intellectual journals, including* Maclean's *and the Toronto* Sun. *Received Canada Council grant in 1974. Nobel Prize nominee for Literature in 1980 after publication of* Confessions, *an epochal study of the use of torture by right-wing régimes. Married (twice).*

W hen Miss Amiel was apprenticing under Toronto *Sun* Editor-in-Chief Peter Worthington to take over his job, poor Joe Clark found himself in a nest of vipers in cold and windy Winnipeg. Saddled with the bruising Progressive Conservative Party leadership review process, the former Prime Minister — who was not even thought worthy enough to be included in the first edition of Debrett's *The Canadian Establishment* — was sufficiently mauled at this Tory gathering that he set in motion the very process of his own downfall. Hundreds of journalists assembled for the blood ritual. And so did Miss Amiel.

Looking back, it is doubtful if any of the activities on the convention floor were more colourful than the deliberations of the Fifth Estate. Mordecai Richler came with a press card and stumbled into the media room looking like the Fourth Horseman.

"Where's Dalton? Where's Dalton?" he muttered to any scribe that passed him.

"He's over there," said someone, who put his hand on

Richler's shoulder and stopped his forward shuffle. "Haven't I seen you somewhere before?"

"I'm Mordecai Richler," he said.

"Oh yah," said the young journalist. "I've read your stuff. Good stuff."

"DALTON!" said Richler when he finally spied the great and mighty Camp. "I need to talk to you. What's going on here?"

Generally, it was an occasion for the media stars to strut their stuff. Hierarchy was based on whether your opinion was worthy of inclusion on *The Journal*, although in journalism's rough and rather wonderful way, this honour dwindled into obloquy when it transpired that nearly everyone who preened his prognostications before Barbara Frum said that Mr. Clark would carry the day.

When the Delphic tally was finally announced and it emerged that a full-scale leadership campaign was on, pandemonium broke out on the convention floor. I was then in a "news management situation," as they say these days, and had the delicious pleasure of dispatching troops which allowed me time to roam wherever the blowhards might wind. There were scrums all over the floor, but the largest and most active one seemed to be near the west side of the Winnipeg arena.

You could tell it was a good scrum. People were five or six thick around the central character or characters; it was impossible from the crush to see who it was. On the outer rim, the gatherers of facts leaned into the crowd to catch the chatter. Some thrust small tape-recorders towards the middle; others were furiously scribbling notes. I drew closer.

At the hub of the throng was Miss Amiel, in her ninth designer outfit of the convention. This one was scarlet with a slit down its back that stopped only a provocative millimetre above her trunk and undercarriage. She was in the midst of an editorial consultation with Mr. Worthington that sounded alarmingly like a fishmongers' scrap. I was too far from the centre to get the drift of the debate. All that came through to the backlines were the high frequency expostulations:

AMIEL: What the hell do you mean . . .

WORTHINGTON: Barbara. For God's sake, if you'd only. . .

AMIEL: Don't patronize me or I'll . . .

WORTHINGTON: I'm not patronizing, but you're being silly because . . .

AMIEL: Are you telling me . . .

WORTHINGTON: Listen. I'm only telling you that . . .

It was all exciting material, I'm sure. At this point I started giving the journalists around me a closer look. *They weren't journalists!* They were all Tory Party delegates festooned with credential badges: from Moose Jaw and Toronto, from Vancouver and Sackville, from Twillingate and Calgary. And some of them were indeed writing down scraps of the conversation, although for what purpose I can't possibly imagine. Maybe simply to report to the folks back home about the big dust-up in Winnipeg.

I walked away as contented as I have ever been, for I had witnessed an historic development in my own profession. Those who had been sent to report were being covered by those who were supposed to be reported upon. All was well with the world.

MAUREEN FORRESTER

Maureen Forrester, CC. Leading contralto and Chairman of the Canada Council. Born 25 July 1930 in Montreal, Quebec. Educated at William Dawson School in Montreal and privately. A long and highly successful career in concert halls and opera stages around the world. Married (separated), with four daughters and one son. Jewish.

In the spring of 1978, the Toronto Symphony made its historic trip to Japan and the People's Republic of China. Maureen Forrester was the featured soloist, but by the time she made it to Peking, this normally good-natured woman was in a state of severe annoyance. Her problem was the Minister of External Affairs, the Honourable Donald Jamieson. The minister was also visiting the Far East and had clearly decided, since his department was picking up part of the tab for the tour, that the orchestra was an appropriate backdrop for his Pacific diplomatic thrust.

Mr. Jamieson, a jolly and good-natured person, is unfortunately cursed with the impression that he is a great speaker. So many people from all walks of life, confusing garrulousness for eloquence, have told him so and as a result he has actually come to believe it.

After listening to three consummate examples of Jamieson windbaggery, Miss Forrester thought she had done her duty. She was thus considerably chagrined when the minister turned up at a special party given for the TS by the Tokyo Symphony, at which Mr. Jamieson was not only unbidden but unwelcome. Unaccustomed as he was to public speaking, he nevertheless decided to hold forth. Miss Forrester fumed and turned to the person next to her:

"My God, that man is a colossal bore."

The person turned out to be Mrs. Jamieson.

When I asked her later what the minister's wife said, Miss Forrester reported:

"Not much. But I rather got the impression she agreed with me."

ROBERT FULFORD

———————◄ ►———————

Robert Fulford, OC. Editor of Saturday Night *magazine. Born 13 February 1932. Educated at Malvern Collegiate (Toronto). First entered journalism in 1949 and has had the usual varied career most journalists are heir to. Among the publications he worked for, before moving to* Saturday Night *in 1968, are:* The Globe and Mail, Toronto Star, Canadian Homes & Gardens, Mayfair *(general interest magazine published in the 1950s),* Maclean's. *He is also established as a broadcaster. Married (twice), with three daughters and one son.*

S mall countries, like Canada, have to take their lumps whether they like them or not. Finland has its Soviet Union, but still managed to produce a Sibelius. Tibet has its China, but still kept the faith. Ireland has its Britain, but still maintained its literary tradition and its bombs. Canada has its United States, but still we have — would you believe — Robert Fulford.

How many years has he been puttering away in his Editor's Column in *Saturday Night?* Not all that long, I suppose, although it seems an age, or more precisely my own era of the Seventies and Eighties. He has the facial features and voice of Uncle Chichimus and if you met him walking on Front Street in Toronto after you had been told he was the repository of the very best that is in Canada, you might well think we were a people of no consequence. This is no Rambo of the North. If he jogs it has had no perceivable effect. This is no contemporary French *philosophe* manning the intellectual barricades of the Old Left or New Right: ideologically, he is all over the map. The Spanish Civil War was not his to fight in and he has never had to stand up against Senator McCarthy or the Central Committee: when he rages, only cultural bureaucrats quake and they have their indexed pensions to soothe their sullied souls.

He is, though, the best journalist in the land and to my mind represents our best side, both to us and to anyone else in the world who cares to take notice. It is the side of articulate concern, common sense and basic decency. This is a vision which only an intellectual in "a country of no great account" (I quote de Gaulle) could bring to complete fruition. Freed from the subservience of having to come to terms with an all-powerful, or waning, or malevolent great power, Fulford the commentator and Fulford the reporter have only the uncertain, often confused and always fractious Canadian national consciousness to fall back on as a frame of reference.

Two leading items stand out in my mind as the major influence in helping me to see him straight. The first was a condescending accolade tossed off in his direction by Morley Callaghan. I had gone to the great novelist's home to interview him on the occasion of his 129th birthday and during the course of a reasonably amiable conversation the subject of Fulford came up.

"You know my son Barry reckons that Bob (Fulford) is the best in his business," said Mr. Callaghan, who smacked his lips in anticipation of his next line, "so long as he doesn't try to write more than 2,000 words. I reckon that's just about right. After 2,000 words, he sort of gets lost."

The old fart. What this means, of course, is that Morley, Barry & Co. go beyond the mundane world of 2,000 words (or less), into the real world of literature. From this I was not only brought sharply up on the prevailing attitude to journalism, but also made aware that that is precisely what Fulford is: a journalist. His job is to be a witness, nothing more and nothing less.

I also remember vividly one of his innumerable two-thousand-worders in *Saturday Night* on the subject of peasant art from the People's Republic of China. As far as I know, he has never been to China and this yarn was written long before it was fashionable among Western intellectuals to point out that everything in the world of Mao Zedong was not exactly tickety-boo. The naive and colourful paintings, which the Chinese Government was for awhile pushing as proof of the liberating winds of the Great Proletarian Cultural Revolution, had been hailed in many Western countries as "wonderfully evocative primitives" that ranked right up there with Inuit carvings and Grandma Moses masterpieces. Fulford's attack point in all this was not the paintings themselves, which, on their own merits no doubt showed a certain and relative imagination and invention. Nor was it even the Communist government of China for, in truth, Western journalists and academics (not to mention their Chinese peers) were several years away from reporting on and analysing the dreadful totalitarian pall that had descended over nearly a quarter of the world's population. Instead, something of the reaction among Canadian viewers of the paintings struck him as fearfully wrong. His learning, which had taught him that there was a two-millenia history and tradition of art in China that had mysteriously disappeared into some sinkhole for over two decades, and his common sense and decency, which reacted violently against the unknowing paternalism and even sniggering among the viewers, conspired together to cause one of those deadly but well-controlled Fulford rages which often adorn the pages of his magazine.

In this light, and despite the then insurmountable ignorance of actual conditions for artists and intellectuals in China, he pinpointed the vaguely perceived horror of the Cultural Revolution and also the woeful and lazy countenances of weekend aesthetes in his own country.

It is much like this on most months in *Saturday Night*. Whether he's having a go at a massive, million-dollar cultural report that somehow misses the whole point behind the word "cultural," or the lemming-like way the national media fell into a trap set by a small-town racist and bigot in Alberta who has now got his thesis (that the Holocaust never occurred) admirably disseminated from coast to coast, or how the nation has abandoned its single most important priority — the duty to educate its children — to the whims of a tawdry political agenda: whether it is any of these things, Fulford struggles to bring the most straightforward, but consistently bypassed, questions to bear and serves them up in a prose style as lucid as George Orwell's and as engaging as Arthur Koestler's.

In an important country, he would have been an international titan because the ambitions and woes of important countries have a bearing and impact far beyond their borders. As our own titan, he represents a lot of the Canadian potential; one we shirk and avoid like the plague. In his columns in *Saturday Night*, we learn to avoid common platitudes but not basic sense. We learn to take a knight's move away from events swirling around us and shed the tempting but illusory comfort of hard-edged ideological positions.

Indeed the thumping he gives to ideology in general may be his most significant contribution to this increasingly polarized world and it surely comes directly out of the Canadian experience, where ideology collapses under the exigencies of regional chaos. He has clearly looked deep into the human psyche. His experience and learning have led him to see what a hopeless hodgepodge we have made of our politics in Canada. There is no safe and sturdy philosophical vantage point from which to charge out in all directions. If you made a chart of all the subjects Fulford has written on throughout all the years of his professional career and assembled them on an ideological scale with pure Left and pure Right at its extremities, you would, as I have said, find him all over the place. You might even think, from such a chart alone, that he was a man of no convictions rather than one of crusading humanity.

Yet it is precisely this trait that engages you from the first sentence to the last, which takes you from a known position into a world that was before your eyes but quite unseen. You may not always agree with the final position in which he leaves you, but you can never go back to what you originally thought. He knows that we are composed in almost equal measures of Left and Right, that the Reagan fan in Vancouver would be outraged if his neighbour had to pay monstrous medical bills because of a fluke accident or tragic illness; that the Sandinista enthusiast in Toronto would be equally outraged if an insensitive central government forced through an urban renewal plan that took no account of neighbourhood views and sensibilities.

It strikes me as significant that Fulford's 2,000 words are about the same length as an average Sunday sermon. In a secular age, he has — consciously or unconsciously — assumed the mantle not perhaps of a vicar but certainly of a moral instructor. Nor are we left bereft of hope or remedy because we have it directly from his own civilizing and sobering line of inquiry that there is a better way to conduct our affairs and thinking. Paradoxically, his method leaves us capable of arriving at different destinations while taking the same route.

I pay no extended tribute to his quirky and delightful sense of irony, nor to his attentive curiosity in the variety of human motivation and action: these are merely the instincts which propelled him into the craft of journalism and which sustain both his interest and his credibility. It is, rather, the dimension of commitment which so distinguishes him and sets him up as a model to all of us who are striving for something more than big bucks and front pages (disdaining neither, I hasten to point out, but not becoming obsessed by them). Fulford has shown his own generation of journalists that in their fixation with other people's actions and intentions, in recording their foibles and their triumphs, the voyeur in all of us can be tempered by committed concern, intellectual honesty and a crusading love for the people around you, whether it is manifested by blistering anger or a just affection for benign follies.

I don't know him very well at all. What I understand is

taken from what he writes — his 2,000 words once a month. I have no idea whether or not he is a religious man (in the broad, rather than the parochial sense). It is therefore completely fanciful that I have come to imagine, hidden above the first sentence of each column, is the ancient priestly admonition: "May the words of my mouth and the thoughts of my heart be always worthy of thee." I do not define the "thee," just the honest voice I fancy is saying it; a voice, I hasten to point out, which can sometimes sound ominously like the honk of a Canada goose.

CONRAD BLACK

Conrad M. Black, BA, MA, LLL. Businessman, author, publisher, Chairman of the board and of the executive committee of Argus Corporation. Born 25 August 1944 in Montreal, Quebec. Educated at Upper Canada College (Toronto), Trinity College School (Port Hope), Thornton College (Toronto), Carleton University, Laval University and McGill University. On the boards of innumerable companies. Author of Duplessis, *the definitive study of the late premier of Quebec, Maurice Duplessis. Columnist for the Toronto* Globe and Mail. *Married, with two sons and one daughter. Religion: papal politics.*

> *High on a hill she stands*
> *Her tower a landmark clear.*
> *Her colours bright are blue and white*
> *To all of her sons most dear.*

It was the fairest of days in the twilight of the Fifties. In the playing fields directly behind the Prep School of Upper Canada College in Toronto, Bob and Chip were beating the living shit out of each other. It was an end-of-year, end-of-Prep explosion and today I'm not sure exactly how it all began. The fight itself I remember vividly. During recess, Bob winged an apple core in the general direction of Chip. Knowing him, I doubt if Bob really intended to hurt anyone, but the apple core nevertheless smashed right into Chip's ear and the fight was on. Bob was the best scholar in the school and a fair athlete; Chip was by far the best athlete and an indifferent scholar. Bob was popular; Chip wasn't. Chip was handsome; Bob had a gangling, warm-hearted face punctuated by a large, discoloured birthmark. They were rivals, of course, but I don't think either they or we understood the dynamics of their rivalry, for they had also been good friends and had even double-dated.

At 13 and 14, we were all ruling the roost at the Prep. Next school year, we would be back at the bottom of the heap when we entered the Upper School and so this end-of-term fight took on symbolic baggage which some of us, even then, could recognize.

"I don't want to fight you, Chip. It was an accident," said Bob, weaving back and forth away from his opponent's jabs.

Mac, the peacemaker, tried to intervene. He and Chip had been best friends only months before, but by the time of the fight had begun to drift apart.

"You bloody traitor," said Chip, hitting out at Mac now. "You're as bad as he is."

And then the fight began in earnest. The entire student population of the Prep was gathered round. Shirt-tails fluttered in the warm, early summer breeze. The smallest boys were in a state of almost sublime ecstasy. Big event. Shocking sight. Factional warfare. No marbles today. Too exciting.

"Hit him. Hit him. Hit him."

Everyone was saying that. Everyone was saying it to Bob. Everyone was against Chip.

At some point during the fight, I found myself standing next to Conrad. We had been close friends earlier, but in the senior year at the Prep we were both in rearranged alliances.

"Look at them," said Conrad. "Don't you want to throw up?"

I looked quizzically at Bob and Chip thrashing about. No. I certainly didn't want to throw up. It was exhilarating.

"Not those idiots," said Conrad, with perfect contempt. "Look at the windows. Our *gauleiters* are enjoying the show. What puppets we are!"

Conrad was right. Most of the Prep masters were watching the fight with evident satisfaction. Blowing off steam, I suspect they were thinking. Conrad ascribed darker motivations to their "voyeurism."

"This place is a concentration camp," he said with his familiar disdain for understatement, "but most of the inmates are oblivious to the fact."

That's the way Conrad talked then. That's the way he talked when he was 10. Big words and strong statements.

As for the slugging match, it would have ended indecisively by the time the end-of-recess bell was rung had not Bob connected with Chip's nose. At the first sight of blood a tremendous cheer went up. The best athlete among us had been humiliated and the dark beast lurking inside all those little bodies was satiated. Everyone, it seemed, wanted to pat Bob's back, to be near him. The wounded gladiator, tears of rage streaming down his face, walked away from the mob and only Wally went with him. Wally put his arm around Chip's shoulder.

Chip went on the play professional football and became an architect who eschewed big buildings and big developments. Bob came back to teach at the college and then went on to be a doctor. Mac is a businessman. Wally embraced Marxism. I'm a journalist. And Conrad? Well, Conrad is still Conrad.

* * *

Sons of a mighty school,
Proudly the palm we bear,
Striving to merit, more and more,
The colours that we wear.

"Look at that jerk Ruffell," said Conrad two years earlier, as we took our recess constitutional around the Parkin Building. "In the real world, I doubt if he'd be trusted to handle paperclips."

Mr. Ruffell was a master. A dreaded master. A known user of canes. I doubt if most Old Boys even remember what he taught them, but some will remember the Claggart-like spell of fear he cast in the classroom. He was in charge of recess this particular day and was chatting amiably with one of the school secretaries. As Conrad and I passed by his shadow, some silly impulsive devil inside me made my voice say: "Old Ruffy seems to have taken a shine to Miss E."

We walked on, giggling as I recall.

With a broad sweep of his right arm, Conrad began one of his special attacks on the school:

"Our pig-stupid colleagues think of this place as the universe," he said. "Why E.P. Taylor could buy up this land and 40 more parcels like it without blinking. These jerks that control our lives are pure flotsam."

"What's flotsam?"

"Garbage that floats on the sea. Did you see what happened..."

This was one of Conrad's few utterances that never got concluded. We both suddenly found ourselves hoisted off the ground by a firm grip on our collars, our toes kicking in the air. Mr. Ruffell had sneaked up from behind and had us both by the scruff.

"What did you two say back there?" he demanded.

With sheer animal fear, I blurted out what I had said, word for word.

"And you?" questioned the blazing master, shaking Conrad.

"I said nothing," said Conrad. I remember the expression on his face being a fairly equal measure of fear and loathing.

"Report to me outside the Headmaster's office at recess tomorrow Fraser," said Mr. Ruffell. "Maybe we can beat some politeness into you."

He let us go and we ran back to our class. It was the first sentence of corporal punishment I had ever received and it was not an easy afternoon or evening that followed. By the time the next day's recess came around and I stood outside the Headmaster's office, I was shaking. Mr. Ruffell approached and put his firm grip on the back of my neck to propel me forward, but it turned out the Headmaster's office was still in use.

"We'll do it tomorrow," he said finally. "Probably do you some good to brood about it a bit longer."

When I told Conrad what had transpired, he shook his head back and forth. "That man is a pathological sadist. He should be reported to the police." Conrad, as usual, was speaking in his overly expansive, adolescent way.

That evening, apart from the enveloping dread, the only thing I remember doing was looking up 'pathological' in a dictionary to see what it meant. The next day I got six swats on the backside, with the last two directly aimed at the back of the upper thigh. I shouted out with pain at those two, but I did not cry in front of him, only later in the washroom. Since I was the first in my class ever to be caned, I discovered within two hours that I could charge a nickel each to a multitude of boys who wanted to see the welts. This went some way to compensate the pain and humiliation.

Many years later, when I recalled this incident to him, Conrad told me that Mr. Ruffell had caned him too. Yet he had never told anyone, not even me.

* * *

Sing of the boys of old,
Praise every famous name.
East, west, south, north,
They ventured forth
And added to her fame.

Memory is notoriously selective. If I set down a list of some of the really dreadful things that happened to me, or which I observed, during the Prep years, I suppose I could make *Tom Brown's Schooldays* look like a tea party. There was old G who used to like fondling boys' ears and backs as he sat on their desks in plain view of everyone else. "Please, Sir, I don't like it," said one latter day Oliver Twist. "Don't like it!?" said old G. "Doesn't it make you feel nice?"

There were masters who pulled boys by their sideburns or, if they were sufficiently bushy, by their eyebrows. Chalk brushes were hurled at our heads by the math master. The science teacher prided himself on the "sporting chance" he gave the miscreants under his charge: the game here entailed placing your hands, palms down, on his desk while he wielded a heavy yard rule. If you pulled them away when he came crashing down, you got off; if he feigned a blow with the rule, however, and you pulled your hands away, you had to go through the ordeal twice, or as many more times as he tricked you.

And yet my memory of those years was of a happy time. Mr. Galt's theatrical productions, Mr. Atack's cupboard of classical records, Mr. LaPierre's scripture stories, Mr. Hearn's wonderful world of English novels and Mr. Gardiner's sex education classes ("Well, you just sort of shove it in there. Don't worry, it always goes in.") In most disagreeable confrontations, I was, I think, perfectly capable of coping by myself. I hated boxing, for example, which in those days we were all required to take part in. I noticed, however, that Mr. Greatrix always stopped any match at the first sight of blood, so the two times I was forced to go in the ring, I took the precaution of so brutalizing my own nose beforehand that a quick blow-out could produce rivers of blood. Hardly a blow ever landed on me before the match was scratched.

This catalogue of corporal and other horrors, long gone from both the Prep and the Upper School, did not, however, prey on one's mind. One simply made do and got by. When I came to work in Communist China for the *Globe and Mail* and people asked me what life was like under the terrible strictures of the dictatorship of the proletariat, I felt I had some kind of peripheral understanding. As boys, we never questioned the authority we were placed under. So far as I know, the only person to do so at that age was Conrad. We accepted the world as it was delivered to us, just as most Chinese had to do under Mao. We also accepted unquestioningly that everything that was done was essentially good in its broadest context, despite the fact that individual acts of unfairness aroused feelings of rebellion. This feeling even continued into the early years of the Upper School, where there was a particularly fiendish French master known to us as the Beast of Belsen. I suspect Conrad assigned that epithet. When a later principal of the college, the kind and decent Patrick Johnson, fired this horror of a sadistic pederast, I can remember feeling real shock. Of course he was a horror, but he was a part of the system. You didn't even think about the fact that he was actually up to no good and could be gotten rid of. Listening to Chinese friends' accounts of their feelings when the Gang of Four was purged, it seemed a mere variation on a well-understood theme.

And, certainly, there was some terrible retribution, again a feature of an unquestioned system in which inchoate rebellion can strike at the most surprising moments. During my days in the Upper School, there was a maths master who was weak and effeminate and made the mistake of trying to be a pal. In his classes, true anarchy reigned supreme. On one occasion, two of the bigger boys — who were by this time 16 and not an insignificant physical threat — held the poor man out a third floor window by his legs as he howled in fear. He never reported the incident, but I was not surprised to learn he became an alcoholic.

As I said, Conrad was the only one I knew who questioned the whole order from a very young age. He was always well acquainted with wealth and power and was often driven to the Prep by the family chauffeur. I believe he always preferred sitting in the back in solitary splendour, but that may be an apocryphal memory. In any event, he had set himself against the imposed Establishment right from the beginning and always resented the power others, like masters or prefects, had over him. In addition, he had a terribly sharp tongue, which is not appreciated in the young. Once in the Prep, a bunch of us, including Conrad, were horsing around in the corridors of the Parkin Building while examinations were being held for Upper

School boys inside the neighbouring classrooms. The main Upper School building had been declared derelict a few weeks earlier and the senior boys, in an emergency measure, had been forced to write Christmas tests in the cramped quarters of the Prep as the main building came tumbling down. The Prep classrooms had large signs on the doors reading: "Quiet. Exams In Progress."

The horseplay must have been making a noisy ruckus because a master emerged from one of the rooms to see what was happening. We were in high spirits and when the master said, "Can't you boys read that sign?" Conrad replied without hesitation, "No Sir, my education here has been wholly inadequate for that task."

You never saw anything happen so fast as the way Conrad was grabbed by his jacket collar, hauled into the examination room itself, pushed down on top of the front desk and beaten within, shall we say, a yard of his life. He deserved some punishment for his cheek and since beating was the norm, it seemed appropriate enough. Because there was such effortless recourse to beating, however, it built within him a terrible sense of rage — which was normal — and a fierce determination to really get even — which wasn't.

During my second year in the Upper School, for example, police were called in to investigate the break-in to a senior housemaster's office. It had been methodically trashed. The housemaster, now dead, was a stern law-and-order man and had been one for some considerable length of time. Indeed, my own father can remember being beaten by him when he was a schoolboy at UCC. Conrad was one of those very special boys who had come to his attention and the housemaster had clearly decided that young Black would learn the error of his ways before he escaped his clutches. How many times he beat Conrad I do not know, but it was a considerable number and each time the stakes for revenge got higher. Neither the police nor the masters ever found out who broke into the housemaster's office, who stole his caning book and who poured ink all over the file where he kept his own private character assessments of the boys. The caning book might have provided the answer, but then it was gone, wasn't it?

When Conrad later staged his notorious exam heist — the biggest single scandal in the college's history — he was not only putting into practice a lot of what he had been preaching all those years; he nearly got away with the ultimate revenge by undermining the entire system of the school, from evaluation by examination to the honour code.

Schoolboy morality is a complex business. When it became known what Conrad had pulled off with two accomplices, he was thought by many to be the cleverest thing alive. To have secured a copy of every single final examination (apart from the Grade 13 exams which used to come, under bond, from the province) represented a considerable act of organization and ingenuity. If Conrad wasn't liked and admired at the school (and he wasn't), he was nevertheless the man of the hour at this particular juncture. His most admirable trait — obsessive loyalty to anyone he likes — was unknown to most. He was simply a very rich man's son who had pulled off a coup. When he sold the exams, he even had a kind of sliding price scale based on his own evaluation. Even then he had developed an encyclopedic knowledge of who was worth what. The conspiracy must have had over half the school population involved. It is a measure of how far we had drifted apart as friends by that time that I didn't know he was involved in the business and only found out when it was too late to make a decision to purchase or not. I suspect I would have bought, especially given the presiding moral atmosphere of the school in those days in which any smart trick against the given order of things was fair play.

When the exam heist unravelled, however, Conrad had a ferocious lesson in retribution and hypocrisy. Those who had been among the most eager to purchase were suddenly transformed into the Knights of New Jerusalem. Overnight he became a pariah and a number of the boys even burned him in effigy on his father's front lawn.

From the fat of Upper Canada College, he was delivered into the fire of Trinity College School in Port Hope. Where formerly he had been a dayboy at UCC and could retreat to the sanctuary of home, at TCS he was a boarder, and not just a boarder but one with a sordid reputation. I gather he did not have a heart-warming experience, although it ameliorated to some extent his earlier views on UCC. The experience also taught him much about the negative rewards of escalation. Revenge can be sweet, but it rarely solves the present and often complicates the future.

Sing of the boys today.
Father in heaven above,
Grant them we pray
In work and play
The strenghtening of Thy love.

TIMOTHY FINDLEY

Timothy Findley. Writer and actor. Born 30 October 1930 in Toronto, Ontario. Educated at Rosedale Public School (Toronto), St. Andrew's College (Aurora), Jarvis Collegiate Institute (Toronto). A charter member of the Stratford (Ontario) Shakespearean Festival, he has performed on both Broadway and London's West End, as well as at drama festivals in Edinburgh, Berlin and Moscow. A successful and critically-acclaimed novelist, his best-selling books include The Wars *(which won the Governor General's Award for Fiction in 1977) and* Famous Last Words. *He has written extensively for radio, television and the stage. From 1974-75, he was Playwright-In-Residence at Ottawa's National Arts Centre for which he wrote the play* Can You See Me Yet? *Divorced.*

God help the critical writing profession if a competent psychiatrist ever decides to undertake a major study of the motivations and emotional landscape of its practitioners. Putting aside much of the crabby, vindictive and whining embellishments as the natural byproducts of overexposure to genial mediocrity, one is still left pondering why on earth anybody would want to go into a business where the principal gratification is a species of sado-masochism of a particularly perverse sort. I speak of my brothers and sisters and from my own experience, for I plied the dear craft for the better part of a decade. Indeed, I do it still from time to time to satiate a dark and hidden lust that knows no name and is shrouded by a thousand sensible arguments on the need — on society's need — for the critical perspective.

In truth we are all critics. The instinct to analyze, to place what we see and hear within the context of our experience, to strut our opinions either positive or contrary, is as natural as sleeping and waking. If it seems fickle and warped for a newspaper critic, throwing out value judgements by the gross, to pronounce that such and such a writer is a genius one day and two years down the road dismiss him as a charlatan ("failed to fulfil his early promise") or rogue ("self-derivative") or beast out of hell ("tenuous grip on reality"), consider merely the analysis true lovers would make of each other upon first consummation; then project it to the divorce court six years later.

So we are all culpable, all critics — from the prophets of antiquity to the shopper fingering lettuce leaves at the grocery store. We will have our standards!

But to write them down and have them seen in print, to build a little cosmology of standards with which to wield the whip or pat the bottom requires a measure of faith or confidence similar to that demonstrated by politicians on their stumps and preachers in their pulpits.

Why then are critics so damn sensitive to criticism? Why do they fail to see any merit whatsoever in an analysis of their own work? Why, when a palpable hit skewers them, do they writhe in agony (and sometimes even phone their lawyers) in ways that most of their accustomed victims would consider unprofessional? Don't look for the answers from the practitioners: their standard response to criticism aimed directly at them is either loathing or vengeance and precludes any rational response. It is a very illuminating experience to hang around the Letters-to-the-Editor department of a major newspaper and wait for a couple of stingers from *vox populi* to come in on reviews written by the staff critics. There is a charmlessly ornate process which often ensues. Copies of the letters are made and sent to the writers. You could lift from the affronted air a dozen choice phrases in the inevitable cacophony which follows: "He's wrong. You can't print it" or "If you're going to print this, you should know I'll be taking legal advice" or "You know who she is, don't you? She's directly responsible for the fiasco" or "I trust you're going to give me a chance to refute this garbage" or (and this one is the killer because it comes bedecked with high moral outrage and a unique strain of paranoia), "Is the paper not prepared to stand by its writers?"

Well, well. . . this is old territory for seasoned hacks. What is perhaps more pertinent than any of the newsroom histrionics is the way in which victims and critics deal with each other. In 1975, when I was still the theatre critic for the *Globe and Mail*, I travelled up to Ottawa to see Timothy Findley's new play *Can You See Me Yet?* Veteran Canadian actress Frances Hyland was in the lead role and the action all took place within the precincts of a mental asylum. Findley had written it while he was Playwright-In-Residence at the National Arts Centre and to the extent that the theatre department there was hoping to establish a solid precedent with this relationship, there were some heavy expectations that came with the production beyond any particular interest in the play itself.

It may be thought disingenuous on my part, but I rarely went to any theatrical offering without high hopes. Perhaps I talked myself into this state of mind, but I feel it was genuine enough. The instinct of messenger to the great unwashed, mentioned above, is as happily coupled with a winner as a prize turkey. The reviewer knows that more people will read his words than will ever see what he is writing about and so a sturdy conceit sets in that the review itself is a kind of performance, usually with deadline pressure not dissimilar to the curtain call.

I hated Findley's play, on which he had laboured for the better part of two years. I hated its premise and I hated its words. To fight it, to beat it down and knock it senseless, I deployed Ridicule and Sarcasm on the left flank, Condescension on the right, and for the main frontal assault I unleashed a pincer attack in which Shame (at the failed experiment) and Feigned Compassion (perhaps the writer should stay away from drama and stick with fiction) combined to effect the final rout. The headline writer back home delivered the *coup de grâce* and by the time it was in print I was already at work on a

Saturday feature, having quite forgotten yesterday's rage. Anyway, within another day it was no doubt wrapping garbage or having wet snow boots placed upon it — such being the ephemeral fame of newspaper writers.

It was not then, therefore, that I paused to speculate on the ramifications for Brother Findley. One assumes there was the usual: anger, disbelief, hurt and so on. I assume it thus because some months later I found myself standing in the foyer of one of the smaller theatres at the Stratford Festival and had the most curious sensation of being enveloped by malignity and seething hatred. Now I have never been a believer in the parapsychological dimension of life, but the sense of being near a hugely inimical presence was so strong I turned around to see who was nearby. That's when I saw Tiff Findley himself, eight paces away and looking in my direction with eyes of fire. We had never been introduced, and I wasn't about to voluntarily walk into the valley of this particular shadow. I have known colleagues who become almost erotically aroused at such proofs of their power, but I wasn't in that sort of mood on this particular occasion. Instead I was bothered by it and troubled by the grief I had obviously caused the man. There had not been anything wilfully malicious in my review of his play, but I had brought my own views on "mental illness" — forged by intimate experience — to bear, and they clashed wildly with his.

In the meantime, Margaret Laurence had written a stern Letter-to-the-Editor defending Findley and the play. When I was shown a copy of the letter, I stormed over to the editor and showed him the program notes of the production in which Miss Laurence had written a flowery and fulsome accolade about the play. I presumed she had never seen it performed, but had written her eulogy based solely on the printed text, ignoring the well-known truth that some plays that have sound literary values are hopeless on the stage, and, indeed, vice versa.

"How can you print that letter knowing that Laurence is

simply a flak for Findley?" I demanded of the editor.

"Easy," he said, for he was constantly bemused by the critics' hyper-sensitivity to criticism, "I just send it down to the composing room."

The play, the review and the letter were all actions which, in themselves, could not be undone. But time, as the presiding physician, can work wonders if hearts will only stay open. Years later, after I had been posted to the People's Republic of China, and after I had gone through the familiar agonies of writing a long book and seen it both praised to the skies and trampled in the dust by my brothers and sisters, I had occasion to visit Miss Laurence at her home in Lakefield, Ontario. We talked about the letter and Findley and criticism. She told me that when she was a young journalist and had written a flashy piece of nastiness, she had received the rebuke of a lifetime from someone she had venerated and the memory of it all still stung. It had, however, led her to consider the consequences of her gift for communication and that this consideration had helped to form guiding principles that were with her yet.

The only way a critic can avoid such consequences is to harden the heart and stiffen the ego. Once the consequences are accepted — both morally and practically — the only way to continue in the critical profession is to acknowledge fallibility and admit your own capacity for pain. The instinct to criticize is very durable and it can withstand an honest conscience. It can even withstand a sense of responsibility without automatically inducing boredom among the readers.

With a greater sense of responsibility, I still don't think I would have liked Tiff's play and I probably would have wounded him in whatever review I wrote. It probably would have made no difference to him, the printed word not always, if ever, being susceptible to the explanations of complex motivation, but it would have added a different, and certainly crucial, new dimension. After the great successes of his recent novels, I met him one day at the home of mutual acquaintances. I told him all this. If I didn't feel I needed the forgiveness he immediately extended, I nevertheless took it because it formed the basis of a mutual friendship and respect which has been achieved at some cost.

LORD THOMSON OF FLEET

Right Honourable Lord Thomson of Fleet, MA. Newspaper proprietor. Born 1 September 1923 in Toronto, Ontario. Educated at Upper Canada College (Toronto) and University of Cambridge. Son of the first Lord Thomson of Fleet and of Northbridge in the City of Edinburgh, he inherited vast holdings in the newspaper business and off-shore oil consortiums. His apprenticeship was held in a wide variety of Thomson concerns. After succeeding to his father's title and holdings, he decided to make his headquarters in Toronto rather than London (England) and has presided over a general expansion of these affairs. Married, with one daughter and two sons. Baptist.

Kenneth Thomson refuses to be called Lord Thomson in Canada, where he now mostly resides, because he considers that the title belongs to his father and has very little to do with him. Apparently, he allows it to be used in England when he is there out of respect for local customs and, no doubt, to honour the memory of his father.

In fact, the son has inherited quite a bit from the father, as anyone who knows his kindly face and is aware that he shops at Toronto's St. Lawrence Market on Saturday mornings can discover. The CBC once did a documentary on the first Lord Thomson and one of the charming vignettes in the show showed the old boy getting measured for his peer's robes at a very fancy tailoring shop, after which he popped on to the London tube and went off to take advantage of a bargain-basement sale of underwear he had noticed in the advertising columns of a competing newspaper.

Back in Toronto at the Saturday market, I have stumbled more than once into the son at the bargain cheese counter:

"Great cheese, don't you think?" he said the first time we met. "And you can't beat the price."

Purchase concluded, he left the premises and went home in his chauffeur-driven Datsun compact.

ZENA CHERRY

Zena Cherry (nee MacMillan). Newspaper columnist and scourge of spouses. Born on an undisclosed date in Prince Albert, Saskatchewan. Educated at Sacred Heart Convent (Prince Albert), Bishop Strachan School (Toronto). Her society and general interest column has been a regular feature at the Globe and Mail *since time began. Member of various volunteer committees, including: Canadian Opera Company, National Ballet of Canada, Multiple Sclerosis Society, Toronto Symphony, Junior League of Toronto. Former board member of the Canadian Red Cross Society. Past Regent of the Lady Tweedsmuir Chapter of the Imperial Order Daughters of the Empire. Founding Chairman of the Children's Theatre. Member of the founding executive of the Committee for Theatre at York University. Director of the Toronto Outdoor Art Exhibition. Four-time winner of the Canadian Women's Press Club "Member's Award." Member of the International Press Institute in Switzerland, Media Club (Canada) and Heraldry Society (Canada). Clubs include: Badminton & Racquet, Canadian, Empire, Garden, Heliconian, Royal Canadian Military Institute and Royal Canadian Yacht. Married, to Wescott Warren Christopher Cherry, now deceased. Anglican.*

One of the biggest mistakes the *Globe and Mail* ever made was to put Mrs. Cherry's photograph on top of her gossip column. Up until that moment, she was a semi-mythological creature that many people really believed didn't exist. In providing pictorial proof of the flesh-and-blood reality, I always felt they undermined part of her clout. Her greatest service to Canadians is to remind each and everyone of them, six days a week, that if they live outside Toronto, they don't really count for much. Every other great national institution based in Toronto is disguised, whether it's the CBC, my own newspaper, the Royal Bank, the National Ballet or the Donner Foundation. They keep fake head offices in other cities, or point to satellite printing plants, or trumpet their national touring schedule: but it's Toronto where they are really found and only Zena has the courage to admit it, glory in it and rub everyone else's nose in it. And so they should be rubbed. Why, when a man is tired of Toronto, he is tired of life itself for there is in Toronto all that life can afford.

Occasionally Zena makes an error, but usually it isn't her fault. She is betrayed from time to time by the people who supply her with information. A good example of this was told to me by Dr. Brough Macpherson, the eminent political economist. Dr. Macpherson is married to the redoubtable Kay Macpherson, one of the great women's activists of our times. Their daughter Susan, a gifted modern dancer, used to perform with the Toronto Dance Theatre and it was on the occasion of one of this company's opening nights that Zena ran up against the Macpherson clan.

Zena and her businessman-husband, Wescott Cherry, had gone to the performance. On the next day she noted the occasion in her column along with the glittering list of other first-nighters. As is the good lady's wont, she listed couples by the husbands' names, and at the end of the paragraph she would incorporate all the better halfs with a catch-all phrase like "and spouses" or "with their wives."

Now Kay Macpherson, I assure you, has never once thought of herself as an "and spouse." Not only that, she and Brough weren't even at the performance. So she dashed off a wonderful Letter-to-the-Editor that began: "O wife of Wescott, mend thy ways." It was one of the best editorial letters ever to be sent to the *Globe* and got pride of place in the paper.

On the following morning, Zena called the Macpherson household to apologize for including their names when they weren't there. Kay was out shopping or campaigning, I can't remember which, and Brough took the call.

"Is that you Professor Macpherson?" said Zena. "Listen, I'm so sorry about the mistake. Those silly PR people gave me the list and I thought they'd have it right."

Brough hummed and hawed politely, because, after all, he is a gentleman and Mrs. Cherry is a lady.

"That was such a clever letter," said Zena.

"Oh," said Brough, "you liked it did you?"

"I thought it was wonderful," she said. "It was so clever I'll just bet you helped her write it."

* * *

Zena's real worth is bound up in her helpless honesty. She may write an up-market gossip column but she has never once pretended, of her own person, to be something other than she was. If some editors of the *Globe and Mail* have solidified their reputations by their ability to spot the spelling errors and lesser *faux pas* of her raw copy, not once in her long career has anyone been able to accuse her of dishonesty — the prevalent trait ascribed by many members of the public to journalists these days. I had occasion to discover this first hand in the People's Republic of China, of all places, shortly after I took up my duties there in late 1977.

Chairman Mao had died the year before and his widow, Jiang Qing — pre-eminent among the Gang of Four — was under arrest. The country had just been launched on its historic opening to the West, although as far as my paper was concerned it had recently taken a giant step backwards by expelling my predecessor, Ross H. Munro, for a series of articles on human rights abuses. During the first few weeks, I was nervous about what I perceived was the precariousness of my position in Peking. This manifested itself in a rather bellicose arrogance when I met Chinese officials because I wanted to show them that whatever they had done to Munro was not going to influence the way I intended to report on events and people in their country.

94

I had spent most of those first evenings in Peking poring over the bureau's files, which stretched back to 1959. During one of those paper rambles, I came across a series of communications between the paper's sixth correspondent, John F. Burns (now with the *New York Times*), and the home office. It was all about Zena Cherry and, six years after the events being described, the pages were still smoking.

This is what happened. Back in 1971 and 1972, the *Globe* correspondent still lived a lonely, isolated life. His ability to travel around the country was severely limited by the machinations of the Information Department of the Chinese Foreign Ministry. Unknown to all outsiders until it exploded into the open, Mao was involved in a deadly inner-party fight with his closest comrade-in-arms and chosen successor, Marshal Lin Biao. The anarchic years of the first stage of the Great Proletariat Cultural Revolution were drawing to a close and the purge of Lin Biao would mark a modest return to a semblance of sanity, symbolized by the re-opening of the Canton International Trade Fair to which businessmen from all over the world were bidden to buy and sell during two hectic weeks.

Thus came to the shores of the Middle Kingdom, unannounced, Toronto businessman and container packaging executive, Wescott Cherry, with his redoubtable wife, Zena, in tow. They visited Canton, Peking and then Hong Kong. Inevitably, she dropped in to a few diplomatic parties and partook of some of the local gossip. She did not, however, find time to say hello to Mr. Burns. After she was out of the country, she wrote about the trip for the benefit of her constant readers in the *Globe and Mail* and the columns were duly printed. I think there was a week of them.

In those days, it took from six to 10 days for the *Globe* to reach Peking, so poor old Burns, the resident correspondent, was unaware of what she had wrought until the moment he was summoned to the Foreign Ministry for a monstrous dressing down.

Was Mr. Burns aware, demanded a seething official, that

"his Mrs. Cherry" had written vicious slanders against the people of China? Was he aware that this poisonous creature from the slimy bourgeois underworld had dared to compare the proletariat city of Canton with the cesspool of colonial Hong Kong — *and found Canton wanting?* Was he aware that Mrs. Cherry had made lewd comments about the women of China in general and Madame Jiang Qing in particular? Was he aware that the people's government was seriously considering closing down the newspaper's bureau for this unprecedented and callous attack?

Poor Burns was in a terrible quandary. When he was finally able to read the articles, his judgement and sense of humour failed him utterly, which was not surprising considering the terrible conditions one was expected to operate under in the Peking of those days. Zena's Chinese columns were nothing out of the ordinary, except that they were set in China. There was the usual list of names, a bit of history, some local colour and tid-bits from the latest chit-chat. She did say that the hotels in Hong Kong were more comfortable and better appointed than in Canton. Indeed they were. She didn't have much of a chance to communicate with ordinary Chinese people because in those days ordinary Chinese people would probably have been arrested for communicating anything more than "hello" to her, so not very surprisingly she got most of her information from businessmen's tales and diplomatic smart talk. It was these same sources resident journalists often used, perhaps with more discretion.

Diplomats told her that, in private, Mao's wife liked to wear dresses, although this was frowned upon for the masses of proletarian women. In her naive and simple way, Zena thought this smacked of hypocrisy, which lots of other people thought too, but she wrote it down as such and had it published. Burns' anger at having someone from his own paper trespass on his journalistic turf was instantly recognizable. He had, however, become a trifle too close to his monumental subject — which happens to all foreign correspondents worth anything — and succumbed to the venomous blandishments of the Information Department.

"Your Mrs. Cherry has undermined all your good reporting," he was told. He should have winced at that indirect accolade from such a source, but instead common sense failed him and his pained letters to the Managing Editor showed that he agreed with the official, although he had a genuine cause for concern if the government was thinking of expelling him not for any of his own merits or perceived demerits, but because of what a bloody gossip columnist had written.

A tempest in a teapot, you think? A footnote from the past and pretty inconsequential at that? That's what I thought when I first read these smouldering letters. I had yet to learn that in China they forget *nothing*.

To celebrate New Year's, 1978, I was bidden to the foreign ministry for an evening's jollity along with all the other foreign correspondents. An evening's jollity with Chinese officials, even in those early improving days, was not exactly a hoedown. It was, in fact, one tension-ridden hour of wooden conversation and mutual incomprehension. It was also my first occasion to meet senior ministry officials and the memory of my predecessor's expulsion was still the talk of the small foreign community.

"You're Mr. Fraser aren't you?" said a middle-aged Chinese in impeccable Oxford-tainted English. His smartly tailored cadre's suit, buttoned high to the collar, bespoke someone who knew how to rise in the system. Somewhat reluctantly, I agreed to the premise that I was who I was.

"Welcome to China," he said, without introducing himself. "Vice-Minister Chen expressed the wish to talk to you. Would you please come with me."

Dum-de-dum-dum, I thought. Now for the next rant about the *Globe and Mail's* sins. I had already had one juicy harangue from officials at the Chinese Embassy in Ottawa who were incensed that Munro's human rights series had been published to coincide with their foreign minister's visit to Canada.

On the contrary, however, Vice-Minister Chen turned out to be the soul of seasonal vivacity. Everything okay? he asked solicitously? Need any help from the ministry? Getting around a bit now and learning about the people and the country? The situation is improving thanks to the downfall of the Gang of Four, haven't you noticed?

Then, in a gesture of formal intimacy, he put his hand on my arm and leaned forward, almost in a conspiratorial fashion.

"How is your Mrs. Cherry?" he demanded in a loud hiss.

"My WHAT?!"

He could not have asked another question that would have dumbfounded me more.

"Mrs. Cherry. Mrs. Cherry. She's a reporter at your paper. How is she?"

"I know who she is," I blurted out. "As far as I know she's just fine. Why on earth do you ask?"

"Ahh," he said, withdrawing his arm and taking a substantial sip from his glass of orange pop. "She is a very brave woman. She came to my country at a terrible, evil time and wrote the truth. She dared to write the truth about Jiang Qing! I think she was the only reporter who ever came here during those years who did such a thing. The Chinese people revere Mrs. Cherry for her courage. She is a model for us."

One lives and one learns. I sent an account of the conversation to my Editor-in-Chief and set about the task of reporting on the land of one billion in a manner that would not detract from the record of a model figure and heroine of the People's Republic of China. I have never knowingly passed over her column since and Dr. Norman Bethune has passed into secondary significance.

KAREN KAIN

Karen Kain, OC. Prima ballerina. Born 28 March 1951 in Hamilton, Ontario. She began her training at the National Ballet School at a very young age, joining the corps de ballet *of the National Ballet Company in 1969. Within one year she was promoted to principal dancer. Since then she has performed most of the principal roles in the classical repertoire all over the world. Married. Anglican.*

The concept of unrequited love has not been much in vogue for many centuries, although it has struck me more than once that the emergence of herpes and AIDS in our own time may bring about a revival of the ancient malaise, the likes of which this tawdry world hasn't seen since the medieval period when allegory was considered a higher delight than consummation. Miss Kain came into my life in late early age when I was manfully pretending that I was a sophisticated dance critic, but in reality was running like blazes just to keep one step ahead of the audience. I saw her from afar at the usual place — on stage — and learned in a twinkling that you cannot be a real balletomane until you are smitten by a dancer, and smitten to your very core.

This complex condition, for which there is no known cure and which spreads throughout the body with a rapidity that would astonish doctors if they could but see it, is not dependent on physicality alone, although I would not want to minimize this element. It is, rather, a synthesis of physical attraction (earthy, inchoate, exhilarating) and imagination (spiritual, specific and sublime). Dance pits desire against control and when you are alone in a darkened theatre, which is to say surrounded by hundreds if not thousands, and the spectre on the stage dances into your consciousness with all her beauty and art, then, Sir, you are a prig and an idiot if your heart does not melt.

Most of her fans, of course, have to behave like silly asses and hang around the stage door for a closer look. I had the privilege of disguising my true intentions behind a mask of semi-official prose. Are her arabesques smartly delineated? Are the *fouettés* executed with effortless precision? Do her haunting arms show to perfection her sturdy classical grounding? Yes, yes, yes. Of course YES, you silly ass. Read between the lines! *You are my ideal, my alpha and omega. Fly away with me and I will take thee far from all this. Dance, dance, dance to your heart's content for me alone. All that is mean, all that is ugly, all that is craven or carnal, all that is petty, all that has nothing to do with us — these I will banish. Let not thy heart be troubled for I alone shall be thy truest protector, thy shield and thy buckler, thy constant companion right up to the vanishing point and beyond . . .*

"FRASER. Goddamn it, it's nearly midnight. Have you got that review finished? You're the last one." (How common and vulgar! At least he can only butcher the printed word.)

I went to her wedding at my own parish church with my beloved wife beside me. Miss Kain married a nice man whom I churlishly discounted that very morning in the newspaper, coming as close as I ever dared in print to tell her of the paragon she had rather nonchalantly passed by. She seemed happy, nonetheless, and my good mate understood. It was not infidelity I was about.

Such purity of heart is not without its traps, for I was later told that Miss Kain can't stand people gushing over her and saying ridiculous things. Indeed, I believe that she first fell in love with her husband-to-be upon discovering that he hadn't a clue who she was.

JOSEPH SMALLWOOD

———————⇥ ⊨———————

Honourable Joseph Roberts Smallwood, PC. Former Premier of New-
foundland and Labrador. Born some time before the turn of the
century in Gambo, Bonavista Bay, Dominion of Newfoundland.
Educated Bishop Field College, St. John's, and the Rand School of
Social Science in New York. Before leading the Confederation Move-
ment in the late Forties, had a varied career in journalism, trade
unionism and enterpreneurial endeavours. Premier of Newfoundland
from 1949-72. Founder and leader of the Newfoundland Liberal
Party. Left Liberal Party in 1972 and founded the Liberal Reform
Party in Newfoundland. Disbanded Liberal Reform Party in 1976 and
rejoined Liberal Party. Author of several books and encyclopedias
about Newfoundland and Labrador. United Church. Married with
two sons and a daughter.

It is no problem whatsoever remembering the exact month
and year the great adventure began. My frontier-defying
mama and I were bumping merrily along the still uncompleted
Trans-Canada Highway of Newfoundland in a Volkswagen
Bug. Since I was about to enter first year at Memorial University in St. John's, the month was clearly September. And since
Smallwood had placed propaganda signs every five miles along
the route saying WE'LL FINISH THE DRIVE IN '65 THANKS
TO MR. PEARSON, it was clearly 1965.

It was so long ago that the only place they told Newfoundland jokes was in Newfoundland. The Post Office on Water
Street in St. John's still divided the mail between "Domestic"
and "Canadian." July 1, as it still remains, was a day of national
mourning, not to keep alive the bitter memories of nearly half
the islanders who were dragged kicking and screaming into the

bosomy embrace of the "Canadian wolf," but to honour the wretched day in 1916 when most of one generation of Newfoundland men were annihilated in a few hours in France during World War One.

If there was any doubt that this was Joey Smallwood's fiefdom, and his alone (and there wasn't), a provincial election less than two years later rather confirmed it. His Liberal Party won 39 of 42 possible constituencies. Since the members' seats in the Newfoundland Legislature are moveable, this remarkable victory resulted in a comic opera setting where three lonely Tories — the sum total of the Official Opposition — sat in grand isolation to the right of Mr. Speaker (the opposite of every other parliamentary legislature in the world, but then Newfoundland has always been gloriously perverse).

Out at Roaches Line, or El Rancho Ersatzo, the self-styled Only Living Father of Confederation held court surrounded by electric-vibrating Relaxo chairs, functioning and broken-down television sets (stacked on top of each other) and the largest collection of books on Methodism in the world. ("See," he would say to astonished visitors as he pulled back a bunch of books from the front of his shelves to reveal even more behind, "two deep".) He was one of the most totally engaging public figures I have ever met and, among Canadian politicians, one of the most utterly ruthless.

* * *

I was always amazed at the dichotomy between Smallwood's reputation on his home turf and the way he managed to come off as an amiable elf on the national scene. Which is not to say he didn't have his fanatical followers on the island, for, as we were told *ad nauseam*, some Newfoundlanders were placed in their coffins with pictures of Joey clutched to their breast. And, for that matter, 39 seats out of 42 says something after nearly two decades in power. What it didn't tell you was the hammer-hold he had over his half-million souls through a combination of blatant patronage, outrageous bullying and the most magical, mesmerizing speaking style anywhere in the land.

How I loved hearing him speak! For two of my four years at university in Newfoundland, I cut lectures regularly to haunt the press gallery of the legislature and listen to him. In the end, I sickened of hearing him twist facts, distort his true and habitually self-serving intentions, and slander — with all the privileges of parliamentary immunity which he manipulated with childlike glee — decent people who had the temerity to suggest that his government might have erred here or there. It is not an easy thing to shed the layers of experience which encrust first impressions, but there was a time when I thought he was the greatest thing in kingdom come.

For starters, he had brought Newfoundland into Canada and thereby fleshed out the map of the Dominion, so that its claim to be a nation *a mare usque ad mare* finally became a fact rather than a wish. Like most Canadian schoolchildren who looked at pre-1949 maps of Canada, the affront of different-coloured Newfoundland and Labrador was as much a presumption to territorial dignity as different-coloured Canada no doubt seems to like-minded schoolchildren in the United States. Anyway, Joey had accomplished the worthy deed and if some of the still-embittered Catholics on the Avalon Peninsula (Smallwood had discovered there were more Protestants in Newfoundland and so turned the Confederation fight into an anti-Papist crusade) regarded him as the negative image of Kwame Nkruma, they managed somehow to drown their rage in a sea of Canadian mother's allowances, transfer payments and federal public works programs.

That's the way I felt for the first two years and the way a lot of mainlanders still feel about grousing Newfoundlanders who hint at separation or wistfully rub together a few coins from the old currency of the Dominion of Newfoundland. Even some Newfoundlanders are turned off by the island national-ism of Premier Brian Peckford, Joey's first legitimate heir since he left high office. Not so long ago, I ran across Harry Steele, the colourful former head of Eastern Provincial Airlines, when he made a flying visit to Ottawa. "Why," said Harry, "Peckford's a complete idiot. He's crapping in the golden trough of Confederation before he's even seen an ounce of oil."

In time, I came to see that Newfoundland's pernicketyness and distinctiveness were an integral — indeed crucial — element in the national fabric, without which we haven't a hope of staggering into the 21st century. Bear with me as I linger on the point.

In Ontario, where I grew up, we longed for a unified nation just like the United States, in which a polyglot society rallied around the central, unifying government and, although small in numbers, by God we would speak as one. In other words, we wanted the rest of Canada to be like Ontario. An exception could be made for Quebec, because Quebec has always been different and anyway Quebec and Ontario have usually understood each other and divvied up the spoils. Everything was fine until Quebec bestirred itself and chose not to be merely a hewer of businessmen and a drawer of priests and backwoodsmen. This development caused — as we all well know — a deal of trouble.

Now who or what saved us from cracking up as a nation? Pierre? Well, he did his bit of course, but the popular view still holds that he caused as much damage as good. Brian Mulroney? Well, he certainly got Quebec's backwoodsmen out to vote when everyone thought they had died at least a century ago, but he's a johnny-come-lately and I'm talking History here. Was it William II of B.C. or the warm reception given to extended French-language rights in Manitoba? One jests. It was Newfoundland of course.

Right from the first day it joined the greater Dominion, Newfoundlanders served notice that the pan-Canadian dream was dead. They got four-sect denominational education enshrined into the constitution. They had already obliterated the indigenous Indian population, thereby cleverly bypassing the land-claims brouhaha in the years to come. They sold hydro-electric power from Labrador to Quebec at such a laughably cheap rate that Quebec can't afford to separate for fear of losing the best bargain on the continent, next to a house in Love Canal, N.Y. They kept on killing adorable baby seals which ensured worldwide opprobrium for Canada. And finally — the linchpin to the argument — they gave us John Crosbie whose first and only budget as Finance Minister brought down a Canadian Government.

Now, do you see it? Without contempt for Newfoundland, the only thing going for us over the past decade was Margaret Trudeau. We defined ourselves by our attitude to Newfoundland, by the very jokes we rolled on the floor over (how many times did you hear the one about the Newfies who lay down in front of an anti-seal hunt helicopter to stop it from taking off?), by the disgust we felt at their reluctance to share oil revenues with us, by the size of their swelling ranks of unemployed, by the pushy antics of young Brian Peckford, by their bad weather, their stinking fish, their crumbling industries. I could go on, but as a unifying force Newfoundland's negative merit has long been established. Moreover, it is a merit allied to our own sense of inferiority, for while our national subconscious told us we were a dull and deedless lot, there were undeniable satisfactions to be had in thinking that we were certainly better than the very least of our parts.

Our pal Joey was brilliant at gauging and exploiting this hypocrisy. On the one hand, he played and replayed the endless saga of the guileless, trodden-upon Newfoundlanders; on the other, he trumpeted the redeeming salvation of "Great Canada" which had offered shelter to the continental orphan from the stormy blasts. Such enticing nonsense, in which mutual self-interest was elevated to the realm of a contemporary Homeric epic, was beautifully deployed during all those early federal-provincial conferences at which Mr. Smallwood hogged the television cameras in much the same fashion that he had taken over the radio microphones during the Confederation debates on the island two decades earlier. Even when we knew he was talking sheer blarney, it nevertheless pleased us to hear it and even stayed our constitution-bored fingers from flicking the channel to *I Led Three Lives* or *Bonanza* or *The Jack Paar Show.* (I travel here quickly through the years of his own media ascendancy.) His energy, right up to the moment that he was laid low by a stroke, was always remarkable and it will always be impossible to forget his blockbuster speeches in Newfoundland during the Sixties.

Like most self-educated men, Mr. Smallwood had read widely and his talks were usually studded with extraordinary little historic or scientific nuggets. Once, he addressed an international academic gathering at Memorial University and regaled it with the wonders which were found inside the rediscovered tomb of the Egyptian boy-pharaoh, Tutenkhamen. Gold and precious stones beyond human imagining, he said, as he catalogued the inventory with the same loving attention a boy counts out his own collection of marbles. He made it all sound good enough to eat or go to bed with.

"But there was something else the archeologists found, something they almost passed by."

Joey paused. He had a roomful of PhDs eating out of his hand. You could see them lean forward ready to munch the next lump of sugar. You could also tell exactly what was on their minds: 'He's a character, alright. A bit rough perhaps, but *what* a speaker, what a man, why he's hardly five feet tall.'

"And do you know what it was they found?" asked Joey.

Hundreds of silent but easily discerned No's filled the hall.

"It was a little bag of seeds. A tiny sack of grains. Do you suppose, thought these brainy archeologists, do you possibly think that if we plant these seeds that anything might grow? What an extraordinary thing it would be, thousands of years after they had been first grown and gleaned and stored carefully away in a pharaoh's tomb, what an absolutely *miraculous* thing it would be if after planting them they were to spring to life and, why, even bear fruit."

You could hear a pin drop. Did it strike anyone there that they probably knew the answer already, the discovery of King Tut's Tomb being a reasonably prominent event in the 20th century? Perhaps because they knew the answer, they became so enthralled and maybe a few were even curious how he was going to relate all this to Newfoundland.

"Well," said Joey, "they planted those seeds and do you know, the miracle happened. The seeds had only been dormant all those years. They only needed the proper nurturing to come alive. How many years had they been in that sack? Two thousand years? (Pause) Two times two thousand years! Forty centuries! Four millenia! Four hundred times ten years.

"Now, in Newfoundland, our island home, in Newfoundland and in Labrador, our great land mass lying on the mainland with Great Canada, we have been like the dormant seeds in the pharaoh's tomb. Not for so long, of course. Just a few centuries, hardly more than four. But we've been waiting to be discovered and nurtured. It was all here. All the potential. All the *capacity* to grow and bear fruit. But we didn't have the means until Confederation. Confederation provided the sun and water we needed . . . "

And he was off, roaring at full speed. He so warmed to this analogy, which I have no doubt came to him at the last possible minute for he only ever wrote down a few notes just before he got up to speak, that he kept it up for the better part of the next hour. Every word was appreciated, every statement believed. They bought the whole bag of tricks, from the miscalculation of King Tut's death to the revised history of Newfoundland, courtesy of J.R. Smallwood. Had he wanted them, he could have picked up a hundred honorary degrees there and then. And these were not dumb Newfies, my friends, but the cream of North American and British academia. Although I had turned off him by this time, I was some proud of him that night. I thought if he could con this crowd, neither I nor Newfoundland need feel ashamed of having fallen under his spell for either part or all of the time.

It is not my aim here to attempt an evaluation of all the controversial aspects of his reign. Certainly he was a significant figure during his premiership and certainly he did some good, although it all seemed to have happened before I arrived in Newfoundland. His major achievements during my time were selling Labrador power to Quebec for a song, encouraging "industrialist" John C. Doyle to dip into Newfoundland's limited treasure-house to his heart's content, establishing an expensive liner-board plant in Stephenville, which went defunct years ago, and promoting the appalling program of resettlement for thousands of perfectly content souls from self-sufficient outports to jobless and dreary shantytowns that were more convenient for the bureaucrats to administer.

Instead, I simply want to embroider the legends of his remarkable style and evoke the flavour of the man in his heyday. He remained unrepentant to the end of his career. Late in life he worked out a deal with a St. John's radio station that each weekday, on his way in from Roaches Line to the Confederation Building, he would stop off at the station and give his thoughts about this and that. It became almost as compulsive listening as Garner Ted Armstrong's *The World Tomorrow,* and I am being facetious about neither: manifestations of megalomania are fascinating to observe from whatever source.

The show was called "Conversation With the Premier" and Joey even provided helpful weather and road condition reports. The radio station supplied a reporter who trooped out of his building each morning (rain or shine) with a tape recorder over his shoulder. Joey would roll down the window of his car and, most mornings, all the poor minion had to do was say, "Good morning Premier. How are you today?" and Joey took up the rest of the time.

The day after he returned from an extensive trip to Europe, he told his radio audience that he had been delighted to accept an honorary degree from a university in West Germany. It was a proud moment for Newfoundland, he said, because he had accepted the honour on behalf of all Newfoundlanders and not just for himself.

The minion, in one of his rare interjections, lushly asked whether the Premier had ever received an honorary degree before.

"Oh yes," said Joey, "quite a few. You know, in West Germany today they think that anyone who has a doctorate is a pretty bright fellow. And if the same fellow actually has two doctorate degrees, if he's that smart, that intelligent, that *brainy*, why they would actually address him as Herr Doctor Doctor . . . Schtukelbaker, say. That's what they'd call him: Herr Doctor Doctor Schtukelbaker. Now if I lived in West Germany, do you know what they'd have to call me? Why they'd have to call me Herr Doctor Doctor Doctor Doctor Doctor — that's five — Doctor Doctor Smallwood. They'd have to call me "doctor" seven times because that's how many doctorates I have."

As I said, I had turned off him by this time. Our last encounter was troublesome and although I blame an editor at the old Toronto *Telegram* for the ensuing fracas, I still feel a slight twinge of professional guilt over the episode.

I had asked permission of my masters to cover what turned out to be Joey's last hurrah, an election he nearly lost outright, the results of which soured his taste for another fight. A few days before the votes were cast, which heralded the end of the long Liberal Party suzerainty in Newfoundland, I travelled out to Roaches Line for a pre-vote interview. He was in the usual form, answering telephones every two minutes, checking the news on radio and television. Throughout the interview, his latest technological gadget — a stereo tape cassette — was blaring forth with international (mostly German) military marches. The only time I remember him standing still was when he was on the telephone and taking notes about this or that constituency which may or may not have been deemed in trouble. For the rest of the time, he marched up and down the living room, not exactly in time to the music, but not far off it either.

"To what do you ascribe the longevity of your political support, Mr. Smallwood," I asked.

He didn't hesitate for a moment.

"The women. Oh yes, certainly the women."

Then he stopped marching and came closer to where I was sitting.

"Look I'll tell you something, but don't for God's sake say I said it. Don't have it coming out of my mouth. I'm giving it to you for background colour. You may have heard a few months ago we had a great Anglican Church congress up in Bay Roberts. The congress opened up with a huge church service and I was invited, as the first minister of the Newfoundland Government, to attend and they seated me right up in the front pew, right on the aisle. Now this was a communion service and the Bishop of Newfoundland was conducting it. You may not know, but in the Church of England, the people taking communion go up the centre aisle and right to a railing before the altar to take the communion. They eat some bread and drink wine, which represents the body and blood of Christ.

"Do you know something quite astounding? The women in that church, all of the women, before they went up to the altar of God, they wanted to shake my hand. Before they took the body and blood of Jesus Christ, they wanted to touch me. Can you beat it? Now don't for heaven's sake have me saying that or people will think I've become too big for my boots."

That, alas, was exactly what I thought he had become and I was in a terrible quandary what to do with the anecdote. On the one hand, I hadn't agreed or disagreed to put quotes around it. On the other hand, I hadn't stopped him. He certainly wanted me to use the story and liked the image it aroused, but if I had done so in the way he fancied, it would have merely been another amusing story about dumb Newfoundlanders. If I put it in quotes, then it would be quite clear what the state of his mind was like after 22 years in high office, but it was probably unethical.

The untidy compromise I resolved to follow was to use the quote, but use it whole hog, complete with the admonition not to quote him. In this way, I felt, the readers of the Toronto *Telegram* would know that the man had turned into something of a monster. They would also be in a position to make a judgement about what I had been about. With a stunning lack of success, I have tried repeatedly throughout my career to let readers know my own prejudices or the journalistic circumstances around which potentially controversial events swirl. It's like a doctor coming clean with his or her patient and not trying to act like God. One is still left being a witness for the readers, but such a policy would also allow them to make a sounder personal judgement about the worth of the witness and the worthiness of the report. I'm sure it would improve the credibility of the press, but the chances of finding an editor who will go along with this are few. Mostly, you will be accused of personalizing your journalism too much, and if not, that it will be struck from the copy anyway as being irrelevant.

And that's what happened at the *Telegram*. The substance of the quote was left in, but the circumstances were edited out. The article was also reproduced in my old St. John's newspaper, the *Evening Telegram*. Joey told anyone who would listen that I was a cheat, a coward, a pimp (for John Bassett presumably) and who knows what else. From his perspective, I tend to agree with him, but my own perspective never got a fair chance.

In truth, while I regret the incident a bit, I am not ashamed of what happened because I didn't deliver up to the sniggering of Toronto yet another stupid Newfie joke. I know of no people I love more, of no place I love better. If they are fools, they are like Lear's good Fool who saw things more clearly and felt things more deeply than all the grandees in the land.

EDWARD JOHN CHARLES SEWELL

Edward John Charles Sewell, BA, LLB. Journalist and former Mayor of Toronto. Born in Toronto, Ontario on December 8, 1940. Educated at local schools and the University of Toronto. Called to the Bar of Ontario in 1967. First elected a municipal alderman in 1969 and was Mayor of Toronto from 1978-80. Defeated in a bid for a second term, he was re-elected as an alderman. He is now the municipal affairs columnist for the Globe and Mail *where he began writing in 1984. Author of two books and numerous magazine articles. Divorced, with one son.*

He was known as "Luke" Sewell at Camp Hurontario and I have no idea where the nickname came from. He was, however, a good counsellor and it was a decent camp, so the combination made for a smashing summer. Not all camps were or are decent. It behooves parents to check them out before they dump their kids for that blissful and childless summer. One earlier camp I was despatched to, based on its reputation when my father had gone there as a boy, turned out to be a sadist's paradise where corporal punishment was always carried out in front of the entire camp population and initiation rites included having to lick the rims of toilet bowls. The owner was on hard drugs and the place ill kept. Most of the equipment and buildings — canoes, sailboats, dining room and sleeping cabins — had bad leaks.

But Hurontario, in Georgian Bay, was a good place and Luke was a fair man, although there were already intimations of the somewhat self-righteous leader who emerged during terse moments at Toronto City Hall. I guess he was about 16 or 17, but even then his sense of democracy was developed nicely. We were encouraged to talk about what we wanted to do and not just ordered around, for he was keen on getting us to decide among ourselves whose turn it was to clean up cabins or carry the heavy food packs across the portages on canoe trips.

In this sense he can be seen as proof of one of the camp's mottoes, which was emblazoned on a beam in the dining hall: IN THE BOY IS SEEN THE MAN. What I want to know, if that is the case, is what happened to a less well-known interest of his. For inside his tent, at all times and hours, he religiously maintained a shrine-like display of photographs devoted exclusively to Brigitte Bardot, whom none of us had ever heard of and whose featured breasts seemed to many of us (at ages nine and ten and eleven) to be threatening/enticing/mystifying.

"Why HER?" I demanded of him one day. My own sister's penchant for Ricky Nelson and Doris Day was tedious enough.

"Because she is the most beautiful thing that was ever created on this earth," he said. And that was that.

In the boy is seen the man, eh?

LAURIER LaPIERRE

Laurier LaPierre, MA, PhD, LLD. University professor, journalist and broadcaster. Born 21 November 1929 in Lac Mégantic, Quebec. Educated at local schools while three degrees were later earned at the University of Toronto (BA, MA and PhD). Acquired his law degree at the University of Prince Edward Island in 1970. He has taught at a wide variety of Canadian universities, including: McGill, Western Ontario, Loyola, Simon Fraser. He is perhaps best known for his appearances on the pioneering CBC Television news inquiry program, This Hour Has Seven Days, *of which he was co-host. Married, with two sons.*

While Laurier LaPierre was working on a doctoral degree in Toronto during the 1950s, he found part-time work at the Prep School of Upper Canada College. In those days, every school day began with a 15-minute scripture reading and discussion class and when I was in the Fifth Form (approximately Grade Six in the state system), he was my scripture teacher. There were not many Jews at the Prep, but S was Jewish and in my class. He was very shy, abysmal at athletics, but an achiever scholastically. I don't think most of us at that age were particularly aware of denominational and religious differences, although one or two had inherited at a young age the prejudices of their parents. I suppose Mr. LaPierre was Roman Catholic and I presume most of the class was Protestant (Anglican, United Church and Presbyterian). In any event, scripture classes were a rather pleasant diversion at the start of the day. No homework resulted from any endeavours in this fruitful field of study and a certain amount of curious disputation was allowed, depending on the adventurousness of the master in charge.

I have a very clear memory of the adventurousness of Mr. LaPierre's classes. Boys of that age much prefer the Old Testament to the New and we were allowed to roam freely through Daniel's Den, Pharoah's Kingdom and Solomon's Temple. When we did veer into the New Testament, as often as not we were directed into the Land of Parables and Miracles. Curiously, the class accepted almost without question many of the fabulous tales of the Old Testament. Moses could part the waves of the Red Sea and turn staves into serpents and this all seemed perfectly acceptable, but let the poor Saviour try to walk the waves or transform water into wine, and our little league of rationalists would blow a metaphorical whistle. We adored stalking around the Garden of Faith with pouting, doubting consciences and hurling unanswerable queries at the scripture master:

"But Sir," we would ask, "if Jesus was so special and could do all these things, why didn't he help everyone?"

It is not for 11-year-olds to remember the answers to such questions; it is enough to recall our cogent skepticism. The charm of Mr. LaPierre was that he treated all such inquiries with great seriousness. If we weren't equals, he nevertheless talked to us as mature individuals and this made all such encounters rather splendid occasions.

Except on the day that Hunter attacked the Jews. I don't recall how the whole affair got started, but I expect we were reading some Bible story in which Jewishness was in the forefront and Hunter suddenly blurted out:

"But Sir, you know what Jews are like."

I don't think I was the only one who immediately looked in the direction of S. You could see his cheeks had flushed red and he kept his head down, looking neither to the right or the left. There was an electric silence in the classroom for what seemed an eternity, when suddenly the scripture master exploded before our very eyes.

"Did you forget Jesus Christ was a Jew, Hunter?" Mr. LaPierre started to get up from his desk and approached

Hunter's desk in such a menacing way, I was sure he was going to clout him to Kingdom Come. But he didn't hit him. He just stood in front of Hunter's desk and roared on and on. I remember the rage, but little of the substance. The letter "H" seemed to predominate: horror, hate, Hitler, holocaust, Hunter, humanity, Hebrew, haughty, humility, hypocrisy. If Mr. LaPierre was not himself hysterical — and he wasn't — he was certainly a man possessed.

The bell rang for the end of scripture class and a new master was at the door waiting to take charge.

"I'll be a few more minutes," bellowed Mr. LaPierre to the uncomprehending teacher who nevertheless sensed the heat of the moment and retreated back to the hallway.

S never looked up once during this scorching 10-minute survey of the history of Jews and Christians. We none of us talked about it during the next recess, or any time afterwards. No one said anything to S or to Hunter. Mr. LaPierre never brought it up again during the rest of the term. But that explosion of rage still seems to me one of the finest and most noble things I ever encountered during those years. It sprang from the very depths and encumbered our young minds with the first inkling of moral responsibility for the words that came out of our mouths.

STEPHEN CLARKSON

Stephen Clarkson, MA, DPSc. Educator and writer. Born 21 October 1937 in London, England. Educated at Upper Canada College (Toronto), University of Toronto, New College Oxford (Rhodes Scholar). Currently a professor of political economy at the University of Toronto, he is better known to a wider audience through his writings in Canadian Forum *and hundreds of other articles and learned papers in various publications. He is the author of several books and once ran unsuccessfully for the mayoralty of Toronto. Married (twice), with two daughters.*

The truly wonderful thing about being in the presence of Stephen Clarkson is that you are made aware, very quickly, that this a Man of Destiny. As with all men of destiny, the world may not yet truly perceive the gift in its midst, but they themselves remain confident that The Truth will eventually out. Whether their causes are big or little, they are all defended and argued from the sturdy redoubt of infallible conviction. If the world is attracted to their ideas and hitches its star to their fortune, then it is seen to have come to its senses; if the world finds the cause absurd and the logic fractured, then that is even further proof of the Man of Destiny's ultimate truth.

Stephen is a kind man when you meet him. He has a catholic range of interests, and a sufficiently novel approach to all of them, to keep you on your toes in any sort of a debate. Around the seedy newsrooms of Toronto, however, he is not taken entirely seriously, especially after his ill-fated attempt to become the Mayor, and his dippy Letters-to-the-Editor tend to confirm prejudices.

Once, after I had written a fairly nasty review of a new play by his friend Tom Hendry, he had been sufficiently outraged to write an equally nasty Letter-to-the-Editor, which was given considerable prominence on the letters page. Hendry's masterpiece was an alternative-theatre costume drama on the life of Lord Byron. The tone of the drama can be taken from the singular fact that the actor who played the title role felt compelled to make his opening entrance each night sporting a perceptible erection through tight pants, although whether this was self-induced or supplemented with stage props was never clear. The play continued in somewhat the same vein thereafter — one of those theatrical offerings newspaper critics light candles in cathedrals for, because they offer us such wonderful opportunities to play Torquemada for a day.

Stephen's letter castigated me for this and that, whipped me for lack of sensitivity, chastized me for missing the lyricism of the language, smashed my knuckles for brutal value judgements, and generally left me in a heap of broken bones and blood-drenched flesh. It was all very bracing. The first intimation of my success came the next morning when I was personally congratulated by the Editor-in-Chief for being the occasion of the silliest Clarkson diatribe in years. The Chief of the Letters-to-the-Editor department thanked me profusely and said he was looking forward to "a roll" with ever-more outrageous utterances from *vox populi* carrying the good fight forward. Fellow critics eyed me with the old green eyes of pure jealousy and the phone didn't stop ringing for days. Not since the momentous day when a half-cracked Toronto playwright had left a dead fish outside my doorway (the Mafia sign of imminent death) had I walked so tall and proud around town.

Several months later, Stephen tried to undermine all this good work of pushing my career along its merry way. I had written a yarn defending the nationalists' cause in theatre as the result of a critical bashing some Toronto plays had received in New York. For this effort, I got a charming personal letter from Stephen saying that I had hit the bull's-eye. He noted his previous attack and, since he is a gentleman as well as a zealot, he offered to write a Letter-to-the-Editor in a similarly con-gratulatory vein as the one he had written me.

Bother!

How was I going to head this one off delicately? Man to man, I thought. I'll just phone him up and explain the problem. Which I did. Except I don't think it came out right.

"Don't be so modest," said Stephen. "I'll happily write such a letter to the paper."

"Oh," I said, "that's incredibly generous, but please don't trouble yourself. It's enough just to have heard from you personally."

"Not at all. I'll write one today."

"Please don't. Please. I . . . I'm afraid . . ."

"What's the matter?"

"Well, you see, it might get me fired."

Being a Man of Destiny, he took it very well, no doubt noting the due effect of his correspondence. But a strange bit of alchemy occurred then, for which I have only a vague explanation. From enjoying the contempt I held him in, I started from that day to like him. Where once I used to snort at his political observations, I began to see them as useful anti-dotes to the status quo. As the intellectual Canadian con-sciousness drifted away from nationalism and high rhetoric, his constancy seemed infinitely more valuable and his unrepentant challenge to presiding orthodoxies a genuinely precious commodity.

George Orwell warned of the dangers of engaging your enemy in civilized conversation. The first thing that you would discover is that the spectre of your animosity was a human being and eventually you would find merit in the very things that were once such a focus of contempt. There are not many Men of Destiny in Canada anymore. The country's imagination is seemingly exhausted and our leaders' siren song is called *South of the Border*. In 18th-century London, when people snickered and snorted at the half-mad poet, Christopher Smart, who was prone to go down on his knees in the city streets and implore the Deity to forgive the erring English and set them upon a truer course, Samuel Johnson once said: "I'd as lief pray with Kit Smart as anyone else in the Kingdom."

God help me, I feel the same way about Stephen today.

NANCY JACKMAN

Nancy Jackman. Women's activist, clergyperson, jeweller, heiress. She is the daughter of the late and legendary Henry Rutherford Jackman, business tycoon and philanthropist; and the sister of Henry Newton Rowell Jackman, chairman of the board of directors of the Empire Life Insurance Company, as well as of Frederic (Eric) Langford Rowell Jackman, president of Invicta Investments and chairman of the Jackman Foundation (among other pursuits). She is daunted by neither of these high flyers, or anyone else for that matter. Unmarried. United Church.

According to her brother Eric, Nancy was the youngest in the family and because of this always felt she had to shout the loudest in order to be heard. When a *Globe and Mail* reporter set about to do a story on this remarkable family — brother Hal is chairman of the Empire Life Insurance Company and has his finger on the pulse of at least 17,000 other businesses; brother Eric is chairman of the Jackman Foundation, president of Invicta Investments, a professional psychologist and defeated Tory Party candidate; brother Eddie is a Roman Catholic convert and priest which, one gathers, did not amuse his staunchly Methodist papa — and it became clear in the ensuing article that Nancy had done most of the blabbing, her mother was somewhat upset. Mrs. Mary Jackman is a handsome and very dignified person and, not surprisingly, didn't like some of her family's foibles trotted out for public inspection.

"It wasn't so bad Mother," Nancy reported later that she had said to her mother. "Think of what I could have told them and didn't."

Well, well. Ms Jackman is a genuine force of nature, and I

have not found her like anywhere else in the world. She is outrageous and generous, considerate and flamboyant; a passionate believer in important causes who puts her energy and money where her mouth is and is a stern champion of her own rights within a family of outsized male achievers.

I know her only slightly and almost entirely from her legendary sorties around and about Georgian Bay; not just any part of Georgian Bay, but the unwelcome-sounding part called Go Home Bay.

At the turn of the century, Go Home became the summer enclave of University of Toronto academics and their families and, to this day, it still retains some of the old connections which have been passed down through several generations. I should state clearly and unequivocally that I only gained entrance to this demi-paradise through marriage. Although I have existed for over a decade in that blissful state I still have the niggling feeling that I am only allowed up there on sufferance. In my old age, I expect my daughters will solidify my uncertain tenure.

My wife's grandfather was Dr. James MacCallum, a pernickety Toronto physician who earned himself a significant cachet in Canadian art history by befriending and championing a young painter named Tom Thompson — and later some of the members of the Group of Seven — through the lean and initially unappreciated years. Dr. MacCallum owned several islands at Go Home Bay and the one on which his cottage was built eventually fell into the hands of Henry Jackman Senior and his redoubtable brood.

Like everyone who has come to Go Home when the sun was hot and the water fresh and clear, the Jackmans succumbed to its lure. On first visit, its rocky islands and rugged shores seem somehow spartan as landscape goes, but it all makes a penetrating and lasting impression. Images of the bay are now part of the national consciousness, thanks to our most famous artists, and, for me, when homesickness hits me wherever I am in the world, it is the memory of a loon's cry, a paddle dipping in quiet, starlit waters, and a pine tree shaped by the west wind that brings on the ache most acutely.

I shouldn't have said "everyone" is thus affected. Although I was not a witness to the event, I have it from extremely reliable sources that Urjo Kareda, the former drama critic of the Toronto *Star* and current artistic director of that city's important Tarragon Theatre, hardened his heart against the place on the only known occasion he ventured forth to this particular hinterland. Like Nancy Jackman herself, Mr. Kareda is a person of considerable substance in matters of personal girth and, while he is undoubtedly fleet of word, he has not normally been able to translate this into speed of locomotion. Except at Go Home and on my wife's island, where a reasonably sized watersnake approached him to exchange notes and was greeted with an approximation of the 100-yard dash. The snake remains, or at least its siblings do, and they are available — at an extremely nominal price — to any actor or playwright who, for any reason, may find them useful.

Ms. Jackman, however, takes snakes in her stride. She is a Go Home girl, after all, and she has an awesome knowledge of the reptilian hierarchy as the briefest of conversations with her immediately reveals. The Pope and his stand on abortion heads the list and you can work your way down the ecclesiastical and political nomenclature until you reach the humble rattler, which she would define as benign and misunderstood.

She is fun to be around because she sets sparks flying. Since she is committed to things, she has a base of high resolve which gives pungent cogency to her talk. God in Heaven knows this only too well, ever since she preached her famous sermon on a fine summer's Sunday at Go Home, a sermon they still talk about with awe.

I only got wind of the fact that Nancy was going to preside at the informal Sunday service the day before it occurred and made arrangements to pick up E and D and take them in our boat to the cottage that had been volunteered for that week's amiable encounter with the God of Nature. I left plenty of time since I felt more than the usual crowd would be out, Nancy being Nancy. None of us could have departed feeling disappointed.

She began *pianissimo* with a prayer for peace, and then went full *forte*.

"As I was sitting on the john yesterday wondering what I was going to talk to you folks about, it struck me that I might not be able to come up to the Bay much longer because some people in my family were trying to make things very difficult."

People leaned forward in their chairs. No one looked to the right or the left. For weeks, gossip had been buzzing around the Bay about Old Man Jackman's last will and testament. It had emerged, after his death earlier that year, that the will was as complex as any of his famous business transactions. No one knew the full details, although D who lived up the sand run, assured me in rather chuckling terms that Jackman *père* had bequeathed the cottage and property at Go Home "to the most deserving grandchild." How this was to be determined, though, was not clear. If true, that rather deftly cut out the son who was a Catholic priest, and pushed Nancy — who has never married — somewhat against the wall.

"I'm not going without a fight," she promised our little congregation and we never doubted it for a moment.

With rather merciless pleasure, she dropped hints here and there of what had been going on, but never enough to piece together a comprehensive narrative. As a device for getting our full attention, however, it was hugely successful and I advise all priests and vicars, high and low, that a little bit of family soap opera could do wonders for their homilies.

Before we moved on to the serious part of her sermon, we were all handed a number of objects. An acorn each, a little pencil and several scraps of blank paper, plus a nail. I can't remember what the rest entailed, but I still have the rough notes I made of the sermon on one of the scraps of paper. In the end, her message was straight from the heart. She seemed to know that we found her intriguing or bizarre or whatever and that she would try, quite openly and honestly, to tell us what made her tick and where the well-spring of her faith was located. As I search the notes today, however, I cannot discern anything beyond some jottings about what we were supposed to do with all our *objets trouvés*. The acorn had something to do with growing into a big oak, although it wasn't as trite as this sounds because I do remember some sensible observations on human development. The nail was a trifle traumatic. At one point we were supposed to push it into the palm of our hands until we couldn't bear it anymore and in this way try to come to terms with some of the real physical torture Jesus had to suffer on the cross.

If I thought this somewhat unworthy and juvenile, it was nothing compared to the panic that spread around the faithful when they learned what they were supposed to do with their scraps of paper and pencil.

"I don't believe in dwelling on my errors and shortcomings in a neurotic and excessive way," she said. But she did believe in confronting them directly, and also in the Christian duty to make a clean breast of our darker, unworthier side.

"Sometimes just the act of writing our sins out acts like concrete enforcement in coming to terms with ourselves. If we just rehearse them over in our minds, there is a tendency to shilly-shally over their significance." We were then bidden to write down our transgressions. D became immediately alarmed.

"What the devil is she going to do with them?" she whispered in my ear. "Read them out? The only thing I'm going to write out is what I think of her crazy sermon."

The worst suspicions seemed to be confirmed when Nancy collected up all the numerous scraps — a few were heavily into self-recrimination — and fondled them a bit too lovingly in her hands. She talked of Christ's promise of forgiveness and, in the same breath, the cleansing power of fire. And then, in a very dramatic gesture, she bestirred herself from a cross-legged squat on the floor and walked determinedly towards the cottage's fireplace. After scrunching up all the trespasses we had done and those, undoubtedly, that had been done against us, she tossed the lot into the grate and set them alight.

Unfortunately, not only was the damper on the chimney closed but there were also some twigs which quickly burst into flames. Smoke lurched out into the room and it seemed much longer than the few seconds it actually took to get the damper open and the smoke headed in the correct direction. D turned to me with unconcealed delight: "Gad," she said, "talk about being all choked up over our sins!"

The service came to an end with an incomprehensible "hymn" chosen from the hideous new joint hymnal of the Anglican and United churches. I can't remember if it was "God of Steel, God of Concrete . . ." or "Now thank we God for bodies strong, vitality and zest . . . and for the sacrament of sex," but it had something of the same gist.

No one lingered for post-service pleasantries. Like me, many of the cottagers had taken notes and were beside themselves with eagerness to get back to their islands and spread the Good News of Nancy's extraordinary sermon. As we went home assisted only by the humble thrust of a 9.9 horsepower outboard, I could see the range of far faster boats darting off in all directions. Within an hour, I thought, the entire bay would be agog with 40 different versions of the sermon. Within a year there were 400.

As I write now, that was eight years ago. This past summer, I am happy to report, Nancy is happily ensconced on her own small island and in a cottage she built for herself. She had just returned from the huge United Nations women's conference in Nairobi and I spied her at a well-attended auction sale at one of the cottages, although I never got a chance for a chat.

"What does that sign mean that was on the side of Nancy's boat?" asked a tanned and tousle-haired kid of his father at the auction.

"What sign?" asked his dad.

"It says: 'If men could get pregnant, abortion would be a

126

sacrament.'''

I didn't hear the response. All I could pick up was: "Don't ask her about it."

In the distance, over the din of auctioneer babble and harmless summer gossip, I heard Nancy's loud and rich laugh ring out like a church bell. She couldn't possibly have heard the father's admonition, but the timing was impeccable. Gloria Steinhem had never been so successfully plagiarized before.

DAVID SUZUKI

David Suzuki, OC, PhD, FRSC. Scientist, educator, broadcaster. Born 24 March 1936 in Vancouver, British Columbia. Spent early years in a Canadian concentration camp with other Japanese-Canadians during the Second World War. Later education at Amherst College and University of Chicago. Professor of Zoology at the University of British Columbia where he has been teaching and carrying out research in genetics since 1969. He has taught and lectured throughout the world and his academic reputation is based on his original work studying the fruit fly. He is best known to the general public as a broadcaster and popularizer of science, notably as host of CBC-TV's The Nature of Things. *Married (twice), with four daughters and one son.*

He was my wife's boss for a number of years when she was directing and producing films for the *Nature of Things*, and I was always attracted by his instinctive ability to take a critical stance at any aspect of the status quo he found around him — in or outside the world of science. Well, no, once or twice the instinct failed him. He was partially responsible for an embarrassingly superficial study of the world of science in China. I was disappointed that he failed to get beyond the perspective of the Distinguished Visitor syndrome to see how horribly science and scientific research had been manipulated to serve political ends.

For the most part, though, he remains one of the most *engaged* Canadians I know. Perhaps his early years spent in a Canadian concentration camp helped to hone his perspective. After he had been awarded the Order of Canada, and just two days after Prime Minister Trudeau had cited him as one of our most distinguished citizens to the visiting prime minister of

Japan, I walked very tall through the corridors of power on Parliament Hill with the great man in tow. I was Bureau Chief in Ottawa for the *Globe and Mail* and Suzuki had been up doing some filming for the CBC. I planned to show him off.

"C'mon and have lunch in the Parliamentary Restaurant," I said. In my fancy, I imagined cabinet ministers, opposition environment critics and science spokesmen lining up at our table for the right to have a few words with the guru of late-20th century sanity.

The corridors of power were slightly less frantic this day. Hundreds of Indian leaders had just decamped after a week-long constitutional wrangle with the Government and there were just the normal number of pork bellies, sycophants, office seekers and rancid commentators lurking in the halls. The great man was dressed in his accustomed attire: neat jeans, open-necked shirt and jacket. We presented ourselves to Monsieur le Maître d'.

Tsk. Tsk. Tsk. Monsieur took note of the Great Man's attire. Won't do at all in the plushy Salle de Subsidized Steaks.

"But I was allowed in here last week when I had lunch with the Minister of Communications," said poor old Suzuki who, like me, didn't understand the difference a week makes.

"Ah yes," said Monsieur to me, as if I should have known better, "but that was when there were a whole bunch of his people here and we lifted the rules. The conference is over now."

We had our pow-wow at the Chateau Laurier instead. A kid asked for his signature and I have not darkened the doorstep of the Parliamentary Restaurant since.

BRIAN LINEHAN

*Brian Richard Linehan. Television personality. Born 3 September 1945
in Hamilton, Ontario. Educated at local public schools in Hamilton
and the Toronto French School. Has a diploma in public relations from
Ryerson Polytechnical Institute (Toronto). Host of the* City Lights
interview programs on CITY-TV in Toronto. Unmarried. Anglican.

I first met Brian Linehan at the home of DuBarry Campeau,
who was then drama critic for the old Toronto *Telegram.* I
somehow found myself in the august position of music and
dance critic seven months after joining the paper and nine
months out of university. The meteoric rise within the editorial hierarchy (straight from the overnight police desk) should
have warned me that the dear old daily was about to go
belly-up before the year was out, but. . . well, everyone is
young and foolish and there's no accounting for self-duplicity
in the world of newspapers and television.

DuBarry Campeau was a delightful creature from some
world far away from uptight T.O. God alone knows where her
accent came from, but as both a critic and a friend her
motivating force was generosity. She disdained neither the
lowly nor the mighty, and if it was true that she had a welcome
ear for a bit of salacious gossip her funniest and most malicious
tales were nevertheless invariably about herself. Mr. Linehan
was neither down nor out during this period in the early
Seventies, but he was certainly far from having arrived
although all the ingredients for his later success were well in
place. The watery eyes and soulful concern, the intense stare
that seemed to plumb the very extremities of the tip of your
soul, the encyclopedic knowledge of the stars of stage, screen
and television. He was young and eager and DuBarry, who was

getting on, liked the young and eager and, more to the point, liked to help them.

No one in the profession who passed by DuBarry's gaze escaped without some measure of her bountiful assistance and concern, Brian no less and no more than countless others. Late in her life, I suppose she struck something of an odd figure to people who didn't know her. Her wigs were always slightly askew and she had certain airs which, if you didn't know her, might have seemed bizarre. Once, shortly before she died, she was served up — skewered and sliced — by the ridiculous "Panache" gossip column of the Toronto *Sun*. It was an unbelievably cruel caricature of her, but she had such a confident sense of where she stood in the universe that she was able to genuinely laugh at it and I loved her instinctive and humble dignity as a human being. She was a gentlewoman, a species unknown to Barbara Amiel or Catherine Leggatt or whichever Sunshine sweetheart used to write "Panache" in those days.

The generosity I spoke of had nothing to do with money, for she had very little of that. It was, as I and especially Mr. Linehan came to know, a professional generosity. If you were new in the business, an introduction to a worthy of the entertainment world was worth its weight in post-1972 gold. Moreover, she had friends all over the world; friends who always seemed to be in the know wherever they were and when one travelled and needed a quick fix on the local scene, the friends of DuBarry always seemed to be primed and willing contributors. To a journalist on the run, to a television moth all a-flutter, this was life itself.

There is nothing nice about growing old, an ancient friend once told me, and I remonstrated with him at such a bleak appraisal. For the young, if they will listen, the old offer a treasure house of experience and insight which leavens all the genius we think we have. More than anything else, they so appreciate camaraderie with the young that they do not even see (or mind if they do see) the constant mining of their rich resources of witness, observation and unalloyed affection.

Few mined deeper than Mr. Linehan, whose little telephone book of significant names, addresses and numbers were studded with the nuggets of DuBarry Campeau. Somehow, however, as he rose in his glittering world, the Campeau rockface seemed exhausted, or not worth the effort, or perhaps merely embarrassing. There were no harsh words between them as far as I could discover. It was simply this: one day she realized she had not heard from him for over a year and it was to be nearly a decade before she would do so again. These were not easy years for DuBarry, although I am not in anyway suggesting that Mr. Linehan was to blame for them. The downside of growing old is, of course, illness and then more illnesses and then death: the prospect of all this concentrates the mind wondrously and, to DuBarry's credit, she shirked the temptation to be depressed and morbid with ferocious courage. Although she liked keeping up with the world of theatre and the media, her name didn't spring to the minds of many editors, not out of callousness, but simply because she was an almost entirely faded presence in arts journalism by then. A modest outlet on a CBC radio panel show gave her inordinate pleasure.

About a year before she died the *Globe and Mail* was planning a special theatre section for the summertime and was in need of freelance contributors, so I mentioned DuBarry's name to the editor in charge. She got two assignments for interviews, one at the Shaw Festival and the other at Stratford. You would have thought I was the Messiah himself from the gratitude she heaped on me, and for which I was entirely unworthy. Her pleasure in doing those two assignments shamed me because I had not done more for her; the lively articles she produced, full of wit and her very own, hallmarked batch of endearing clichés, brought home how much more she could have contributed to our paper had we been more astute.

Yet she never, at least not in my hearing, complained about fate or fickleness. Not even when the phone rang at her home one day and it turned out to be Brian Linehan's secretary. Mr.

Linehan, it seemed, had lost his private telephone book and it was nowhere to be found. Could she, DuBarry, please give the secretary the phone numbers for all their mutual friends and acquaintances?

I don't know what she did in the end and apparently Mr. Linehan then called himself, which was decent of him. All I ever heard from DuBarry was: "Well, he's done terribly well. He's right at the top of his field."

A gentle woman.

CHARLES RITCHIE

Charles Stewart Ritchie, CC, MA. Author and diplomat. Born 23 September 1906 in Halifax, Nova Scotia. Educated at Trinity College School (Port Hope, Ontario), University of King's College (Halifax), Oxford University, Harvard University and Ecole Libre des Sciences Politiques (Paris). Honorary degrees from six universities. First joined the Department of External Affairs in August, 1934. Successive positions include: Third Secretary, Washington Embassy (1936); Second Secretary, London High Commission (1939); First Secretary in London (1943); First Secretary, Ottawa (1945); Counsellor, Paris Embassy (1947); Assistant Under-Secretary of State for External Affairs, Ottawa (1950); Deputy Under-Secretary (1952); Ambassador to the Federal Republic of (West) Germany and Head of Military Mission in Berlin, 1954; Ambassador and Permanent Representative to the United Nations, New York, 1958; Ambassador to the United States (1962); Ambassador and Permanent Representative to NATO and the European Economic Community, 1966; High Commissioner to the United Kingdom, 1967; Special Adviser to the Privy Council, Ottawa, 1971. Author of: The Siren Years, An Appetite For Life, Diplomatic Passport and Storm Signals. Married. Anglican.

Although Mr. Ritchie is thin and tall enough to look like a Canadian version of Ichabod Crane, he carries this precarious frame about the world with charming dignity. And there is such a sparkle in his eye, containing equal parts of naughtiness and affection, that it is impossible not to be impressed simply by his mere presence. Unless, of course, you are the desk clerk at the huge and unwelcoming Sheraton hotel facing Toronto's City Hall.

It was at an event of pleasing self-gratification for dozens of Canadian writers. Billed as "The Night of 100 Stars" and maliciously sub-titled by some as "The Night of 100 Hacks", McClelland and Stewart Publisher Jack McClelland had flattered a sufficient number of scribes' egos to get them out for a gala evening of fund-raising for some undoubtedly worthy cause. It's hard to think of who wasn't there. Margaret Atwood and Robertson Davies were in attendance, along with Peter Newman and Conrad Black, Tiff Findley and Harold Horwood, Farley Mowat and Margaret Trudeau (the author), Phyllis Grosskurth and Gary Lautens — oh, it went on and on and none looked more eminent than Charles Ritchie, festooned with all the bric-a-brac (medals, orders, insignias) of his long years in high office.

Yet when I ran across him, he was clearly a deeply troubled man.

"They won't let me into my room," he said with a nervous laugh. "I've had enough of this lot and I want to go to bed."

"Why don't you use your own key then?" I asked, but it was the wrong question and I was late in catching up to his splendid agony.

"But that's just the point," he said in utter exasperation. "I left the damn thing in my room and they won't believe I am who I am."

"That's ridiculous. Let's go to the front desk."

"It won't do any good. I've already tried."

We went anyway. I had never heard anything so ridiculous.

"Look here, my man," I said to the snip of a lad who had been left in charge of the desk, "this is Ambassador Charles Ritchie. Will you please give him a key to his room or make arrangements with the floorboy to let him in? He's left his key inside."

I was not prepared for what ensued.

"Listen Buster," he said to Mr. Ritchie. *To Ambassador Ritchie.* He who was wearing the Order of Canada around his neck. He who had dined with monarchs, presidents, field marshals, cardinals, Nobel laureates and Rocket Richard. He who had to separate Prime Minister Lester Pearson from the menacing bully-boy grip of President Lyndon Johnson during a fearful altercation at the White House over the Vietnam War policy of the United States. He who had figured in one of the great literary romances of our times, with the English writer Elizabeth Bowen. *Buster?*

"Listen Buster," said the clerk. "You can bring anyone up here who you want and they can claim you are Marilyn Monroe for all I care. But as I told you before, I'm not giving out another key to that room unless I see some identification. Those are the rules and I'd get fired if I did anything else."

"Look here, my man, watch your tongue," said I, putting him smartly in his place for taking such a shockingly irreverent tone to such a Hyperion as he. "Ambassador Ritchie, show him a credit card or something from your wallet."

"But that's just the very point," said Mr. Ritchie with even more exasperation, "I left my wallet in my room. I don't have anything in my pockets."

With that he went through the motions of going through all the pockets of his dinner jacket again.

"Hold on! Hold on!" he said in triumph. "Here's something."

He had reached deep into an inside jacket pocket that was clearly not his accustomed place to leave anything. His tall frame was almost bent over double as he wrestled with the formidable garment to retrieve something the tips of his fingers had trapped. Out came a piece of paper.

"Aha," he said with genuine vigour as he slammed the paper onto the clerk's counter. The young man approached it with some caution, perhaps aware that this tale's ending was soon to come. He picked it up and perused it back and front.

"It's a cleaning ticket," he said in disgust, "and there's no name on it."

"But the address, the address," said Mr. Ritchie, whose brief moment of confidence had quite collapsed. "That's my address in Ottawa."

"Listen buddy, how do I know where you live?"

Buddy! Where are they training these cretins today? *Buddy* to him who knew Churchill and de Gaulle, to him whom Mackenzie King was just another pushy politician. *Buddy!*

"Alright my man, enough of this nonsense. Fetch the manager." I was as calm and in command as Monty in the desert: I'd wrangle with Rommel and no one else.

"Oh good idea," said Ambassador Ritchie. "I should have thought of that myself. The manager will solve all this mix-up."

"Don't count on it," I said. "He may have trained the kid."

When the night manager finally arrived, no doubt after a full briefing from this ridiculous creature, I noticed that the glint of Mr. Ritchie's medals caught his eye. Obviously he would be terrifically embarrassed.

"What seems to be the problem gentlemen?" he said, but it was not asked in a friendly manner. "Do you two fellows want a room together for the night?"

Now it was my turn to be outraged. With as painfully condescending a voice as I was capable of summoning, I explained the dilemma to him. If prisoners at Kingston could be kept in as adeptly as this guest was being kept out, solicitors general of Canada would need no sleeping potions at night.

Perhaps as I went through the tale, and there was now an audience of some six or eight people around us, the night manager's heart began to soften. I told him about the gala evening in the ballroom. That, if necessary, I could get the Governor General of Canada himself to come up and vouch for Mr. Ritchie's identity. Finally, he held up his hand:

"Okay, okay. I figured out a way."

He directed the cretin to fetch Ambassador Ritchie's check-in card.

"We have a sample of his signature on the card and if he writes it the same way, I'll give out a key."

A piece of paper was put on the counter and a pen slapped into the great man's trembling hand.

"What do they want me to do?" said Mr. Ritchie.

"Just sign your name sir and then everything will be okay."

He scrawled out his moniker and it was handed to the night manager, who held it up against the hotel's card. His eyes widened a little and then he gave the two specimens to the cretin for a look. To my consternation, the little twit started shaking his head negatively. Then he showed the two signatures to me and I had to admit they seemed a trifle different. I looked into Mr. Ritchie's face and was about to start laughing when I saw quite clearly how alarmed and upset he had become by all the nonsense. The night manager must have seen the same thing because at long last he relented. He even called him "Sir."

"Maybe we better go up to the room, Sir," he said. "I'll take you up."

As we parted at the elevators, Ambassador Ritchie turned to thank me. He has lived a full, sufficient and wonderfully varied life and it was nice to see a bit of the spark come back to his eyes.

"I succumbed to thinking I was something special down there," he said gesturing vaguely in the direction of the still raging authors' party. "This was damn good preparation for the day I meet my maker."

PIERRE ELLIOTT TRUDEAU

───────◁ ▷───────

Right Honourable Pierre Elliott Trudeau, PC, CH, QC, MA. Lawyer. Former Prime Minister. Born 18 October 1919 in Montreal, Quebec. Educated at Jean de Brébeuf College (Montreal), University of Montreal, Harvard University, Ecole Libre des Science Politiques (Paris), London School of Economics. Called to the Quebec Bar in 1943. Joined Privy Council Office in Ottawa in 1949 as an economic and policy adviser. Began practicing law as a labour and civil-rights specialist in 1951. Appointed associate professor of law at the University of Toronto in 1961. First elected to the House of Commons in 1965. Appointed parliamentary secretary to Prime Minister Lester Pearson in 1966. Minister of Justice in 1967. Elected leader of the Liberal Party in 1968 and was Prime Minister from 1968-79 and 1980-84. Has received numerous honorary degrees, freedoms of cities and peace prizes. Made Companion of Honour by Queen Elizabeth II in 1984. Married (divorced 1984), with three sons. Roman Catholic.

Kipling assures us "The tumult and the shouting dies," and eventually "the captains and the kings depart." The true nature of the fraudulent rancour that surrounded the final years in office of Prime Minister Trudeau can be taken from the unearthly silence which so happily crowds his life today. Among despised democratic leaders in the Western World, the British can still work up a healthy lather about Neville Chamberlain and in the United States Richard Nixon is a byword for this or that. Now that Mr. Trudeau is in retirement, it is almost easier to push the button of vituperation on poor old Mackenzie King than the Jesuit of Sussex Drive.

Why is this? Why should someone who roused the deepest cynicism in the media and brought forth howls of outrage from the masses as they watched him thumb his nose in nightly

30-second news clips be allowed to escape into private anonymity? The answer is depressingly simple and is to be found
mostly within ourselves. The incalculable hopes with which
we invested him in 1968 were bound, by the laws of contemporary media-induced public consciousness, to lay him low
before we were done with him. This is a trite and well-known
psychological reality, but the balm of quiet which surrounds
his person and name today is a trusty indication that we never
hated him as much at the end as we thought we did.

I think this is because he is a good man, a decent man. By
this I do not mean that he did not err. The catalogue of his sins
during 12 years of close scrutiny is widely available in a variety
of forms. Our own sins, which are probably no worse or better
on a relative scale, stand beside them, but are mute because
that is the way we would have it. We expect those we set in
charge of us to be better than we are and, since this is
essentially illogical and impossible, the disgust and repugnance
we usually come to feel for our leaders is a kind of self-hate.
Mr. Trudeau's biggest image problem was simply that he didn't
seem to give a damn about it all. When we compared what we
expected of him in 1968 with the venal politicking of the late
Seventies, he emerged as the very personification of Beel-
zebub. The collective memory of the nation is very shallow.
The dear old pre-1968 dominion that this monster pillaged and
raped didn't seem quite such a blissful place at the time. If,
however, we start from 1968 with no expectations about the
benefits of philosopher-kingsmanship, then it can be seen that
in real values — and I do not include the soaring deficit as
anything worthy of being included in "real values" — there
hasn't been a hell of a lot of change for the worse.

The country is still together, which, considering the roller-
coaster ride it had, is no small statement. Our government still
gets elected by the universal franchise. We are still lazy
workers and imperfect nationalists. More people are unemployed, that is true, but revolution in the streets has been
thwarted by our comprehensive safety net. We eat and sleep

140

well. Train travel continues to deteriorate. A case could be made that we are marginally more tolerant towards minority groups, but I wouldn't want to push this too hard for fear of spoiling all the fun for the National Citizens' Coalition and Barbara Amiel. Over this rather stable progression from 1968 to 1984, we allowed Mr. Trudeau to prey on our minds to the extent that we could not judge the man or his actions rationally. Even his dwindling stock of admirers, ever faithful to the inchoate image of 1968 (which never had much grounding in reality either), found themselves damning him through apology and omission. He was a cardboard cut-out figure when he started his ascent in national politics and we dressed him in rich clothing. With a self-righteous anger, not unlike that summoned up by Colonel Dreyfus's commanding officer when he tore the epaulets from the unfortunate man's shoulders, we tried to disgrace the Prime Minister in our minds in every way possible. I admit that when he had his terrible troubles with Margaret, we were officially on his side, but this support always struck me as rank hypocrisy. His good lady had gone too far, too fast. We preferred our more cautious demolition: it was measured and even stately, and while we positively trilled to the extraordinary gossip leaking out of 24 Sussex Drive — trilled? I devalue the memory, for it was orgasmic — we did have our standards. We would vilify him our own way, not hers.

All his nastiest traits were duly reported, analyzed, and eventually bound up in the books of Walter Stewart and Richard Gwyn. His more tedious side was inadvertently preserved in George Radwanski's epic tome. I haven't much more to offer here except some anecdotes from my own peripheral encounters with him. Try as I may, all I ever discovered was a human being. A captivating, humorous and considerate human being too, although this no doubt was a carefully concocted ruse for, in truth, I was a very important person when he first had the pleasure of my company.

St. John's, Newfoundland: 1968

Outside the Newfoundland Assembly, the weatherman's prediction had come true: wind, fog and rain. But then it was still winter and that was a safe prediction for most days in St. John's. He came out of the mist, transported there by a government-issue Chevrolet, but he was wearing his green leather coat and rakish fedora. The man on the moon? Not at all. Justice Minister Trudeau had flown in from Ottawa to explain his new bill that would take the law out of the nation's bedrooms. Alas for him, he did not know the nation would be rummaging about in his own bedroom a decade later. No doubt power corrupts, but whom exactly does it corrupt?

An odd assortment of layabouts from Memorial University, myself in their ranks, had cut classes to see this strange creature we had only just begun to start interesting ourselves in. The late teens are a superbly giddy age for political discovery: so much tolerance, so much logic, such sensitivity to nuance and detail. Anyway, we liked him straight off because he didn't seem to recognize the Premier-for-Life, Joey Smallwood, at first glance. Good sign. I'm sure no one remembers a word he said that afternoon in the legislature, but we nevertheless clung to all of them at the time. It was high-polish stuff and considering the sloth and venality of the later Smallwood legislative assemblies, it might just as well have been St. Paul talking to erring sinners in Corinth.

After he finished, he left the bar of the House and took a seat in the special visitors section below the galleries, where the rabble was assembled. I leaned over the balcony to get another look at him. At that same moment he looked up and broke into a wide grin. A great grin. To me it translated thusly: Isn't this a lark, what did you think of it all? Afterwards, we crowded him in the corridors and prevented Papa Joe's henchmen from whisking him directly off to the Premier's office. He was content to banter and peppered us with questions about our studies, about justice, about the provincial

Liberal Party — well, we never got beyond that point for we had too many horror tales to report — and the henchmen soon realized it was time to make their move against us and our libels. Off he went to the political bed Joey was even then getting ready for the two of them. The corners were all neatly tucked in, and although the bride flirted right up to the final leadership convention vote some months later, he never actually put his head on the pillow. In later years Joey always felt betrayed by Trudeau, but that was because he tried to push the flirtation too far.

"I admire Mr. Smallwood's energy," said The Man on the eve of his election as party leader and prime minister. He left unsaid the fact, which was obvious to Memorial students right from the beginning, that he couldn't stand the smell of the old buzzard's breath.

Wakefield, Quebec: 1971

The wife of the then President of the Treasury Board, C.M. (Bud) Drury, was dying of cancer and the Prime Minister and his wife had decided to come and visit her at the Drury's chaotic and welcoming version of the Ponderosa in Wakefield, outside Ottawa. Mrs. Drury is properly remembered as one of the great animators of Ottawa. She loved young people and, even more, she liked helping them in their various endeavours. If the Prime Minister of Canada was going to come and pay this very special courtesy call, there were certainly some people who should be around to take advantage of it. Before she had done with the arrangements, family friends like my sister and I had been invited, along with nearby relations of French-Canadian staff, a bright (if eccentric) securities analyst from Montreal, and of course the whole Drury tribe: two sons, two daughters, sons-in-law, grandchildren, hens, dogs, cats, rabbits, etc.

Mr. and Mrs. Trudeau motored down in his Mercedes sports car from the Prime Minister's country estate at Harrington

Lake. They arrived, trailed by a carful of bodyguards, in the early afternoon. It was a glorious summer's day and the little lake on the Drury property glistened and beckoned. Mrs. Drury, dressed in a housecoat, presided over the events from a lawn chair overlooking the lake. It seemed to me that she had decided the only way to make sure the whole event didn't devolve into a mawkish concern for her current plight, which she had accepted with courage and occasional sardonic humour, was to keep everyone busy. Margaret Trudeau at this point was pregnant with her first child and was put on a chair next to Mrs. Drury where she proceeded to sulk for most of the time. That's ungenerous. I'll correct it. Mrs. Trudeau was shy and had difficulty communicating with others.

Part of the problem may have been the simple fact that her man was down on the dock carrying on like a 16-year-old lunatic. The Drury boys tried to outdo him on the highboard with jack-knife dives and double turns, or whatever the silly things are called, and he bettered them every time. We laughed at each other till our sides split. The Prime Minister was high as a kite from facing the physical challenge of youth, and we were even higher having such exclusive proximity to him. Later, in the small changing room, all the men were crowded together as we put on our clothes. Mr. Trudeau had had a set-to with Opposition Leader Robert Stanfield in the House of Commons the day before, which we had all read about in the papers, so when I saw him in his jockey shorts the mouth that not even good taste and decorum can shut up suddenly said:

"Aha. American shorts, eh? Can't bring yourself to wear an honest pair of Stanfields?"

He looked at me with bemusement. The Stanfield family business was always good for an arch joke or two. "Now I know journalists are supposed to be observant, but don't take it to extremes. Actually, on my honeymoon (they went skiing in British Columbia), an aide managed to sneak two pairs of Stanfield longjohns into my suitcase."

"Did you wear them?"

"Are you kidding?" he said. "You know very well you can't give any quarter in politics. As for the aide, he hasn't been heard from since."

Montreal, Quebec: 1974

It was intermission during a performance of Les Grands Ballets Canadiens that I had come to review for the *Globe and Mail*. In the VIP foyer at Salle des Arts, where the critics and special guests of the company had gathered, I saw him away in the corner talking animatedly to a bunch of ballet groupies. I sauntered over towards them to eavesdrop, when I heard him give an analysis of the first ballet that was as good as anything I was going to be able to come up with. He has a seemingly instinctive skill to get to the heart of a problem with an adroit question for which he clearly knows the answer, but with which he solicits genuine debate. It is, I know, part of the formal process of Logic, but he always seems to do it with grace and style, even when he has no intention of changing his mind.

When we finally talked, he learned for the first time that I was the dance critic for Canada's national newspaper. I could now fill this book with the names of important journalists whom he was introduced to during his political career and claimed never to have heard of. He clearly never had any sense whatsoever of the flattery which we consider our due. In this he was the antithesis of someone like Brian Mulroney, or even Henry Kissinger. The good doctor came to Peking once and solicited the advice of three or four journalists who had been invited to have lunch with him. What lap dogs we turned out to be! You do not have to bribe your average journalist with money and perks. On most occasions, all you have to do is take him seriously: that's more than enough expenditure to buy yourself onto the front page.

Mr. Trudeau, as is known to some, is a dance fan. A former dancer with the National Ballet had told me of classes he and

Pierre had taken together in Montreal during the Forties. Right there and then I decided this would be a great occasion to make a pitch for an interview based on his balletic past.

"C'mon, c'mon," he said. "We can't do that. I've got enough problems with the West as it is. But you, tell me about you. Is this your job, travelling around the country and taking in all the dance?"

I could tell from the tone of mock admiration that this was what he wanted my job to be, so I didn't bother him with the details of late-night editing and fighting the mournful feature ideas of the assistant editor. "Sure," I said, "that's it. That's all I do."

The bell went to summon us back to our seats.

"I want your job," he said. "Right now."

I trust all this now puts into a far happier perspective his later and allegedly disrespectful pirouette behind the Queen's back. When the band plays, a guy's gotta dance.

Peking, China: 1978

On his fourth trip to China he came all alone. Out of office and with a rebellious beard shrouding his high Asian cheekbones, he had arrived in Peking on the same day that Richard Nixon and Edward Heath turned up. Nixon was there to bask in the friendship of the only country that didn't despise him in his great disgrace. Heath had fancied a look at Tibet, recently opened to outsiders, and from which he had just returned. Trudeau was on his way to Tibet at the suggestion of his friend Arthur Erickson, the architect, and with whom he teamed up in Peking.

"What's this," I said when I finally caught up with him. "You, Nixon and Heath have all been rejected by the masses, yet the three of you turn up on the same day in Peking where you all plan to meet with Deng Xiaoping who is back in high office after being purged three times. Is there some sort of seminar for the dispossessed going on?"

He loved it and later, when he returned from Lhasa and met Deng, he used the line to solicit the old man's advice for out-of-work leaders.

"What did Deng say?" I asked.

"He smiled," said Opposition Leader Trudeau, "and advised patience."

I knew he would be given a tightly controlled look at Lhasa, so just before he and Erickson departed for Tibet, I snuck a special map of the miraculous city into Erickson's hands. I had just come back from the place and knew exactly the sorts of things which would interest them. The map showed where the army headquarters were, for Tibet then was still an armed colony and Lhasa has more Chinese residents than Tibetans. I also showed how they could work their way through the maze of lanes and alleyways of old Lhasa and pointed out the little second-hand stores where they could purchase wonderful old Tibetan artifacts, which were so different from the garbage the Chinese authorities were pushing in the state stores.

Talk about gratitude. The two of them used the map to escape their Chinese minders and had a high old adventure. Their government hosts were totally mystified at their prior knowledge of Lhasa and the thank-yous I received on their return to Peking fixed in my mind that there was a favour to collect if the political climate should ever turn propitious for him again.

I was also very proud of Trudeau on that trip. Nixon had come to be stroked and left without a ripple. Heath, suffused with self-importance, went to Tibet, where Britain once had considerable interests and responsibility, and took it upon himself to congratulate his Chinese hosts on the good things they were doing, stubbornly oblivious to the atrocities which had been perpetrated on the Tibetan people since 1959. But Pierre Trudeau, freed of the etiquette required of a head of government, asked one of his devastating questions for which the Communists had no answer:

"How long," he asked, "do you think you will need so

many troops to control and contain a minority people?''

Ottawa: 1980

Fate is sometimes a humorist. The patience advised by Deng Xiaoping was needed for less than a year and, after announcing his retirement, Mr. Trudeau found himself back in office. Later I heard Mr. Deng was talking about his own retirement and I wondered who was teaching whom the summer before. I found myself in Ottawa as acting Bureau Chief, with debts of gratitude in the bank.

"Remember the map?'' I wrote in a saucy letter to Mr. Trudeau. "I'm in Ottawa now and I need guidance. How about an interview?''

He gave it to me, good fellow, but I heard from my spies that what he really wanted to do was send me a map of Ottawa pointing out all the secret places like the Sparks Street Mall and Rideau Hall. It was the first and only interview he granted to the *Globe and Mail* while he was prime minister. He loathed the paper and eventually, editorially, it reciprocated.

London, England: 1985

He came back here as a free man. He walked along the Strand and through the buildings of the London School of Economics, reliving earlier student days. He saw old friends and made some new ones. He went to the theatre. In all of this, and even later when he went to Paris to see the stage musical Napoleon, I am unable to report any signs of *ennui*, regret or longing for his former office. Maybe they are there and well-disguised, but after a great long talk the only impression I was left with was of a man who had loved living the very day which had just passed. Nothing more, and certainly nothing less.

ALLAN FOTHERINGHAM

Allan Fotheringham. Columnist, author and troublemaker. Born 1932 in Hearne, Saskatchewan. Educated at University of British Columbia and University of Toronto. He has had a varied career in journalism and worked for several newspapers and magazines, notably the Vancouver Sun *and* Maclean's. *Married (and divorced). There are persistent rumours that he is a member of the Jehovah's Witnesses.*

Slam and slash journalism is not really the rollicking and cheery pastime many of the uninitiated seem to think it is. As with critics, a psychiatrist could have a field day examining the neuroses and insecurities of some of our most savage public commentators.

Like any other human being Dr. Foth has had his fair share of grief. Because of the nature of his business, however, only his closest friends will provide a comfortable shoulder during rough times. For the rest, colleagues and readers alike, a Foth hit may be palpable and hugely enjoyed, but any hurt that comes his own way is equally pleasurable and well-deserved. The man, therefore, walks an emotional tightrope. He knows that many of even his most enthusiastic fans are watching his performance with the same sort of ambivalent fascination as the good folks who troop out each year to see the air show at the Canadian National Exhibition. There's always the chance of a crash.

Val Sears, the caustic political writer for the Toronto *Star*, is perhaps the ace squelch artist in the country. Moreover, he has not boxed himself into a stylistic corner like Dr. Foth, who allowed this to happen as the unavoidable price of his considerable success. One gathers Mr. Sears has long harboured less than fraternal feelings for Dr. Foth, which makes the following encounter all the more mysterious.

Let us turn back the clock a short time to the Ottawa Press Club in the wee hours of the morning. Dr. Foth is in a relatively good mood, without the least hint of becoming tired and emotional. He is, however, about to make a very big mistake. He has been busy soliciting his colleagues' opinions on the advisability of moving his satiric base from Ottawa to Washington, a very big change in direction for a journalist who has been such an effective Fool to Parliament Hill's Lear. Most of us say what is expected of us. "Sounds terrific," or "It should be a stimulating challenge."

Over in a quiet corner, Sears is nursing his drink. You'd only offer a penny for his thoughts if you were a masochist or had won the DSO at Verdun. Dr. Foth approaches, hesitates and then puts the query to Sears. It was folly even coming close:

"Why Al," said Sears, with the warmest of hail-fellow-well-met smiles, "you've got a really good gig going for yourself up here. Everyone things you're the Wizard of Oz. Take your act to Broadway, though, and you're dead in a night."

There was no verbal reaction. Dr. Foth just melted away, his shoulders noticeably sagging. One smart blow to the solar plexus of his psyche had wholly winded him, where all the huzzahs collected during the previous half-hour had been dismissed as merely his due.

Sears looked mournfully into his glass. "Silly ass," he snorted, talking to no one in particular. "What a silly ass."

RICHARD SADLEIR

Richard H. Sadleir, MA. Principal of Upper Canada College. Born 23 April 1929 in Toronto, Ontario. Educated at Trinity College, University of Toronto; Trinity College, Oxford. English Master at Upper Canada College from 1956-63. Dean of Men, Trent University, 1963. Master of Peter Robinson College, Trent University from 1964-69. Vice President and Associate Professor of English, Trent University 1969-75 when he was appointed Principal at UCC. Married, with one son and two daughters.

It is always amusing to read articles, learned or otherwise, on the sociological implications of Upper Canada College. This is not because they are necessarily wrong, but unless they have been written by one of the creatures who actually went through the dear place they always seem to be invested with far too much seriousness — either in delineating what a perfidious and iniquitous place it is or in exaggerating the worth of the Establishment connection.

In Communist China there are several so-called "key schools" in the Peking municipality. They cater exclusively to the brightest and the best, except that there always seems to be a rather large number of children of the well-off official class filling the desks. Many of them are neither bright nor among the best of anything, but their well-placed papas have real clout. It was always thus and always will be. At UCC brains and "a good attitude" certainly have their roles to play in student selection, but in the end — and despite a heartening increase in the number of academic scholarships — it is still papa's clout (i.e. cheque book) that makes all the difference.

Until a few years ago there was no qualitative difference between the education one got in state-supported schools in

Ontario and their private equivalents. I should know as I went to a fair number of them: Oriole Park Public School, UCC, Oakwood Collegiate Institute, Lakefield College School (well before Prince Andrew and the heir to the throne of Spain ennobled its then charmingly run-down premises), Jarvis Collegiate Institute and — just because I loved Grade XIII so much I elected to do it twice — Jarvis Collegiate Night School.

It would be nice to report that this catalogue of the Ontario school system showed evidence of a precocious childhood devoted to earnest studies of various educational methods. It was, alas, rather closer to a combination of Sloth and Woody Allen's experience at eight high schools: they were all for problem teachers. Well no, not all the teachers. Indeed that's why Richard Sadleir is in this book. If we're lucky, all of us carry a memory of a good teacher who ignited something or other in us at an early age. I had a few at various of the above-listed establishments, but Mr. Sadleir was the first and perhaps because of that he seems to shine through the most.

He was a young English master back in 1962 and hung out in an absurd classroom located in the basement of one of the boarding houses or residences. This leaky, subterranean locale, which even Tom Brown might have rebelled against, was in use because the entire main building of the Upper School had been declared in danger of imminent collapse and ordered down. Between the destruction of the old and the construction of the new, there were two years of incommodious hustling between dreary basements, windy portables and tiny desks in the Preparatory School classrooms. Mr. Sadleir was still a bachelor then and had a reputation for being a trifle severe or cold or distant or whatever term one used for masters who didn't immediately suck up to the boys (the yukkiest sort) or beat the livingjasus out of them (like S, the sadistic French master, who should have been had up on criminal charges years ago).

Now this was education before William Davis' revolutionary reforms were first unleashed, reforms which managed within one generation to put Ontario at the very head of Third

World educational systems. (My 13-year-old nephew's spelling errors are today pronounced "phonetically sound" by his teacher and blame is instead cast on the idiocies of the English language, the only mother tongue he'll ever have.) In addition to whatever inspiration I got from those English classes in the basement, we were all required to learn a fair deal by rote. Hardly a week went by without having to reproduce huge swaths of Shakespearean poetry or fifty rhymed couplets courtesy of Alexander Pope or entire poems by Robert Frost. These hated exercises in regurgitation have been with me ever since and my gratitude for them, for the models they sent winging around my brain, is quite literally incalculable. I learned to build a "memory palace" in these classes, places to house scraps of fascinating facts and trivia. In each "room" there was a dresser where you could pull out a drawer to find just those things one needed in the spur of the moment, like two minutes before a deadline or far away in deepest China, where the only reference materials were a security pass and the latest copy of the *People's Daily*.

I remember Mr. Sadleir telling me that if I learned the sequence of English kings and queens, and their dates — by rote — I would be able to place each period of literature and the respective writers in their proper sequence. The drawers of the dressers in the memory palace soon filled up with all sorts of other wonderful things simply because it existed and was capable of constant replenishment. He never called it a "memory palace." I only learned years later that this device of memory storage and retrieval was Jesuit-inspired in an adaptation from the Greeks. But it was the same system I learned and sometimes, in a fanciful moment, I wonder if that isn't the heaven itself I'll go to when death arrives.

Thinking back to his classes, I cannot recall much of the particular substance of his talks. Perhaps they were far more mundane and ordinary than nostalgia preserves, but there was no doubting the atmosphere. The combination of respect and fairness was unbeatable, especially considering the alterna-

153

tives. The respect was necessary because, in those days at least, a master who could be had by the boys was immediately rendered useless as a teacher.

Fairness, though, that was a novelty and Mr. Sadleir's matter-of-fact fairness provided the first lesson I ever had of how an essentially totalitarian institution could be transformed into a democratic one. We were studying Dickens' *Tale of Two Cities* and, typically, were rather more curious about the bestial conditions inside the Bastille than the nobility of Sydney Carton. During the week we discussed the novel, I came across an article on the Bastille in an arts magazine my parents subscribed to called *Horizon*. The author had done a study of the prisoners and the conditions in the Parisian fortress-prison at the time of the French Revolution and his findings showed that life inside wasn't all that bad. Indeed, for the aristocrats, it was rather pleasant because they were allowed to bring in with them many of the creature comforts they desired, including servants. I brought this up during the discussions and Mr. Sadleir, for whom this was an entirely new thesis, didn't care for it very much. He heard me out, but then said:

"Sounds to me like a fancy version of *Mad Magazine* you've been reading."

The class thought this was hilarious and I could feel the blood rising up inside me. My ears were alight. First of all I had been trivialized and made the subject of mockery. Secondly, it had been done by Him on whom my schoolboy adulation had resided. Lord, was I angry!

That night I got out the copy of *Horizon* and a sheet of my mother's best notepaper. I tried out seven drafts of a letter to him, ranging in mood from the nonchalant to the vicious. They were spread out on my bed and I finally chose Number Four as it seemed to me to have just the right amount of respect and irony (14-year-old version, that is).

"Sir," it began logically, "I thought you might be interested in seeing my fancy version of *Mad Magazine*. Fraser. P.S. I believe it has all the proper sort of footnotes."

The next day I waited till recess when he was out of his classroom to leave the magazine and note on his desk. Triumph with vindication was only an English class away! When it came, it was no less sweet than I imagined. He actually apologized to me, read portions of the article to the class (I had no need to take notes, naturally) and then carried on rather extravagantly about *Horizon* itself.

"The Bastille article is fun," he said, "but what I was really grateful to read was Walter Kerr's essay on *The Merchant of Venice*. I've never felt comfortable teaching about Shylock and I've never felt very easy about such a great man as Shakespeare writing such a role."

Kerr's thesis, a summary of then recent Shakespearan scholarship, essentially advised those who felt queasy about the anti-Semitic aspects of the part to consider the social and historical background of the Jews in Shakespeare's own lifetime. First of all we would discover that, considering the times, this may have been the first arguably sympathetic deposition of a Jew on the English stage ("Hath not a Jew eyes . . ."), and also that when Shakespeare was writing there might not have been more than a dozen Jews in the realm.

I am not pushing this thesis and, indeed, I may have got the gist wrong. What I remember vividly was the honesty of a school master who could admit to his students that there were things he didn't know and things left to learn. I was flabbergasted. And he did it in such a way that we all learned something from the exercise.

The bell went to end class and life returned to normal.

"On a scale of one to ten in brown-nosing, Fraser, that rates 15."

"Suck eggs, Deeks."

"It's okay," said the funniest friend I had there. "Haven't you noticed. He got so excited he forgot to give us the memory test. Keep up the good work."

RICHARD HATFIELD

Honourable Richard Bennett Hatfield, PC, MLA, BA, LLB, LLD. Premier of New Brunswick. Born 9 April 1931 in Woodstock, New Brunswick. Educated at Acadia University and Dalhousie University. Called to the Nova Scotia Bar in 1956. Executive Assistant to the federal Minister of Trade and Commerce from 1957-58. Sales manager Hatfield Industries from 1958-66. First elected to the New Brunswick legislature in 1961. Elected leader of the New Brunswick Progressive Conservative Party in 1969. Has been Premier since 1970. Unmarried.

Whatever he eventually decides to do with his life, or whatever the voters of New Brunswick decide to do with it, Richard Hatfield already stands convicted and condemned (of an "irregular lifestyle") in the High Court of Public Opinion. Few danced in the shadow of his troubles with more glee than some of the journalists he had befriended in years gone by, and if the hubris-hounds are correct in thinking there is justice in the saga, it is even more necessary to remember the forgotten or unreckoned qualities of his character that encompassed kindness and generosity, loyalty and forgiveness, gregariousness and altruism.

Unique among Western politicians, the Dalai Lama said of him after a meeting that he had met few people with such a restless soul in search of a sturdy home.

ROBIN PHILLIPS

———————◄ ►———————

JOHN HIRSCH

———————◄ ►———————

Robin Phillips. Actor and director. Born 28 February 1942 in Hasle-mere, Surrey, England. Educated Midhurst Grammar School, Sussex. Theatre training began at the Bristol Old Vic Theatre School. First professional appearance was as "Mr. Puff" in The Critic *(1959). He moved to Canada in 1973 after having established himself as an actor on stage and screen and a director, also for both media. Artistic director of the Stratford Festival (Canada) from 1974-80 and artistic director of the Grand Theatre in London (Ontario) from 1982-83. Unmarried.*

John Hirsch, OC. Theatre director. Born 1 May 1930 in Siofok, Hungary. Educated Jewish Gymnasium, Budapest; and St. John's Technical High School, Winnipeg. A director of international renown, his productions have been seen throughout North America in particu-lar. He is a former head of drama at the Canadian Broadcasting Corporation and from 1980-85 was artistic director at the Stratford Festival (Canada). Unmarried.

T hose who know either or both of these two brilliant stage directors will wonder by what provocation I am moved to join them together. There's a very simple answer: in my own mind, they are as inseparable as Rosencrantz and Guildenstern. In saying this, I am not in any way trying to suggest that their well-known antipathy for each other is irrelevant. Rather it is precisely their antipathy which has bound them and which, being young and foolish, I once managed — like Alice, innocently but curiously, walking through the looking glass —to get caught up in.

But first, let me actually be provocative. Consider the quite astonishing similarities between the two men:

They are both men of the theatre.

They were both born outside Canada and share the generous and inspiring faith in their adopted country that the native born have such a difficult time summoning up.

They were both highly controversial artistic directors of Stratford.

They share similar lifestyles.

They are both plotters and schemers.

They are both loyal (in their fashion).

They both arouse the strongest passions in other people.

They are both restless.

They are both endlessly sensitive to criticism.

They are both natural traditionalists and inventive innovators.

They are both geniuses.

And, as noted, they both hate each other's guts.

I got hit in their crossfire in 1977 during my waning days as a theatre critic. Robin was still artistic director at Stratford and had invited Hirsch to be a guest director during the season. To service the established ritual of advance articles, I had travelled to Canada's own version of Bosworth Field to interview John and, once there I did a very stupid thing. I believed a fib without checking it out. Well, perhaps it wasn't a fib, but it was certainly a bad misunderstanding. During the course of my conversation with John, I irritated him by mentioning some of the talk around town about the pressure Robin was putting himself under by personally directing so many productions while also trying to oversee the festival itself.

"You haven't fallen for that guff, have you?" said John, who, as a former artistic director of Stratford (and who would

158

go on to become one again) talked with authority. He told me that directors get paid a set sum for each production they do and that no one in Stratford's history was cleaning out the till more efficiently than Robin. That, in any event, was the clear implication and it left me terribly upset.

Phillips seemed to me, still does in fact, a wonderful *arriviste* on our shores. He had to suffer the predictable slings and arrows of bruised nationalism because he wasn't born in Mimico, but he weathered all that admirably and stuck to his guns. If this or that production struck some people as being off, or even struck me that way, his cumulative effect was awesome. The excitement and dramatic controversy (the life-blood of theatre) he brought to Stratford was so palpable you could have sliced and packaged it. The intensity of his own personality and the commitment he forced actors and designers — and, God knows, audiences and critics too — to give him were new elements in Canadian theatre, at least for my generation and those coming up. That was a remarkable achievement and no one can take it away from him. Because of the intensity, however, he was personally the source of very remarkable scrutiny and gossip. I met no one who was indifferent either to Robin or to what he was doing at Stratford.

When it was suggested to me that the vision of this hard-working and increasingly pale man was something less — that crass, commercial considerations should have been at the root of our chagrined sympathy — then I felt cheated and didn't see why the wider public and especially the cohorts in Stratford shouldn't know. But I did it all wrong. I thought this information might be thought a trifle tasteless if it came out of Hirsch's own mouth, so I made it my own information. Never doubting its veracity because it came from a former artistic director (who, no doubt, operated under the rules he assumed Phillips was following), I committed the cardinal journalistic folly of not checking the point further.

I've never had quite as speedy a reaction to a story before or since. Shortly after 6 a.m., which must have been about 10 minutes after the *Globe and Mail* was delivered to Stratford, the phone rang in my Toronto apartment. How long it was ringing before I woke up I don't know, but I let it ring on for at least 20 times and then staggered into my study to pick up the receiver and bang it down at the same time. There, I thought, that will teach that bloody publicist to call me at this hour. Ten seconds later it was ringing again.

"Hello," I snarled angrily.

The voice didn't identify itself, nor did it seek confirmation that this was indeed the home of the jolly, peace-be-to-all-your-homes critic of the *Globe and Mail*.

"Where the fuck did you get that bit of insane shit you published today?"

"Robin?" I asked, knowing full well who it was. "Robin? Is that you?"

"I'm asking you where the hell you got that fucking libellous garbage you wrote."

This was something more than a cold shower. This was seething like I had never heard before.

"Now what are we talking about?" I asked, stalling for time so that I could at least get two wits together.

"Don't give me that fucking bullshit. You know exactly what the fuck we are talking about. About your fucking article in the fucking *Globe and Mail*. It's fucking shit, shit, SHIT and I warn you I will not take it lying down. People are reading it around here already. I asked a secretary to come in early to help me this morning as a special favour and she had read it. She just looked at me as if I was the most miserable, craven bastard in the world. Now who the fuck told you this fucking lie?"

I did have the presence of mind to reflect, for half a second, that a man who was surrounded every day with the beauties of Shakespeare's language seemed to be remarkably dependent on one word. What about cur, or varlet, or a whole catalogue of Falstaffian invective?

"I think, professionally, that I mustn't tell you Robin, but you're a smart man and can figure it out. It was, as you no doubt already realize, from someone who knows about such things from experience."

"The fuck he does! I'm telling you I'm not leaving this one alone. I'm going to take it up with our board and you'll be hearing from us very soon."

With that he hung up abruptly and I didn't even have a chance to say, "Have a nice day." I learned later that his next call was to John Hirsch and I would have loved to be on the party line to that one.

Double, double, toil and trouble. There was no getting back to sleep. At noon, I went down to the paper and explained the mess to the Entertainment Editor, the Features Editor, the Assistant Editor and finally, Old Glory himself — the Editor-in-Chief.

"Well, we'll wait for developments," said Old Glory. "Sounds like they'll be coming very soon. You thought the politics of theatre would be easier than dance, didn't you? This is all good experience for your China posting."

Funny man.

Within an hour, the wintry blast of Hecuba came from Stratford in the form of a Telex letter from the chairman of the festival's board. The charge of undue profit for extra productions was mercilessly exposed for the cowardly libel it was and confirmed by quotations from Phillips' own contract. I agreed (as if I had any choice) that the letter must be given due prominence on the letters page and I asked to be able to write an article correcting the impression I had left in our own section. This was a businesslike piece and stated that the claim was erroneous and based on an unfortunate misunderstanding. Obviously I kept Hirsch out of it. I had made the decision to use the item and keep it outside quotes — and had failed to check it out.

Time passed. I had a lunch with Phillips and we squared away any outstanding grief that remained between us. I even ran into John during a play intermission after I got back from China and he apologized to me for "inadvertently leading me astray.''

In retrospect, of course, it was a minor squabble, born aloft by the feverish excitement and flash tempers of a new season. For someone who really doesn't like ferocious quarrels, private or public, I seem to trip over them all the time. From this I have had to learn to accept that great artists really do have more licence for outrage than ordinary people. When I was a dance critic, I despised Rudolf Nureyev's appalling behaviour to fellow artists and to minions dependent on his goodwill. What right, I used to think, does someone, who has been given such extraordinary gifts, have to carry on like a lunatic and exceed by a country mile the bounds of normal behaviour and basic decency?

The answer is that they exceed here to almost the same extent that they exceed in their talent. It doesn't forgive or excuse miserable behaviour, it only explains it. God help them, it may even be a crucial element in their particular genius which, when worked out on a stage, ennobles us all. In any event, it is not for a newspaper critic, who has the easiest revenge of all a mere deadline away, to stand in moral judgement.

ROBERTSON DAVIES

Robertson Davies, CC, DLITT, FRSL. Author, journalist, actor, educator. Born 28 August 1913 in Thamesville, Ontario. Educated at Upper Canada College (Toronto), Queen's University (Kingston) and Balliol College (Oxford). Sometime actor at the Old Vic Repertory Company in England, he returned to Canada in 1940 as Literary Editor of Saturday Night magazine. He became editor of the family owned Peterborough Examiner in 1942. The only true Renaissance Man Canada has ever produced, his prolific writing output includes essays, plays, novels and gaudy scripts. He has been showered with awards and honours and the occasional bad reviews, which he takes like a cat to water. He was the founding Master of Massey College at the University of Toronto and now holds the title of Master Emeritus of that institution and Professor Emeritus of the University. Married, with three daughters. Jungian.

The beard, the books, the manner, even the very gait: Robertson Davies had long ago brought all of them into a unified whole that, to an outsider anyway, transformed a shy and easily wounded man-boy into a significant totem of the literary and academic establishments. It was not the translucent fraudulence of this role that seemed so appealing at first. Within seconds of meeting the Eminent Fellow, it was clear that if you pricked him he did indeed bleed. He has chosen for himself a hard role, one that arises from natural instincts and inclinations, but which nevertheless pushes him into situations I suspect he would wish to be light years away from: love of audience is cancelled out of loathing of close scrutiny; the compulsion to create is battered about by another's compulsion to desecrate. Master Davies is a wizard, a weaver of words, a consummate thespian in everyday life, something of a god in journalistic integrity (and he was a journalist for many, many years), an alchemist capable of brewing dark potions of irony and revenge, a teller of wild and wonderful tales, a legend in his time. He is also a very human being and there's the only real rub.

A few years ago, *The Journal of Canadian Studies* devoted an entire issue to a critical celebration and examination of the works of Robertson Davies. Although it came with lumps and warts closely observed, it was on the whole, not only laudatory but also a rather joyous hosannah of thanksgiving for the presence in Canada of such a singular sage and character. Master Davies was formally asked to write a short preface to these various works, including an essay which examined the images of cruelty to be found in his more famous books.

The Master was neither amused nor gratified by the invitation to preside over this critical banquet at which his soul was carved up to provide all the courses. It was, he said, like asking the goose at the Cratchit's Christmas party to say grace before dinner.

Criticism! How fearfully second-nature it is. We are all of us ready to apply the whip when it suits our fancy, doling out our approbation only when a mood of well-being and sufficient self-confidence has brought to the fore our few ounces of generosity. Those who attack the most, like the easily conned con-artist, are the most susceptible to the twist of the knife. Years of professional experience make not one whit of difference.

I had, for example, returned from China to Canada in triumph. The posting had gone well and a successful book had been well-received — and had even made me prosperous. My employer offered me the chance to write a thrice-weekly column on anything that came into my head. I should have sensed the danger then, for far too much comes into that overburdened receptacle. I did not think about this assignment. I did not plot or plan. I just started writing and it was an absolute disaster for months. (At best it was scatty, at worst unfocussed and rambling.) Not until I sat down and worked out a specific set of objectives, narrowly defined and rigorously adhered to, did the column take on any form or force; but by then readers and colleagues had already made up their minds.

At the time the experience was absolutely horrible, although today it doesn't pain me at all to write about it. I learned a great lesson about public writing in the daily press: start off loud and brassy for a couple of weeks and you'll never look back. Readers make up their minds about their messengers very early on in their assignments and they rarely retreat from first impressions. Halfway through the initial misery of writing the *Globe's* national column, which seemed to me at the time akin to what it would be like trying to make love to a woman whose idea of foreplay was to review — adversely — the previous night's efforts, I was not of a mood to take much criticism. During tough times, one builds a shell for self-protection and while it can be easily shattered, the process of rebuilding it occurs almost as quickly.

The only thing that still rankles in my mind was that I had exposed myself to the brickbats of some of the prize assholes in my business. There was Peter Worthington in the *Sun* bemoaning the loss of early promise, or his colleague Douglas Fisher pointing out that "even good writers don't necessarily have the ability to write good columns." Through the mail, my chum Urjo Kareda informed me in three sweet sentences that my friends were appalled at the spectacle of my transformation into an "up-market Joan Sutton."

It was in the midst of these cheery accolades that I had occasion to run across the Master. We bantered on a bit about this and that for awhile and then he said:

"I read your column without fail . . ."

He paused and I knew instantly that he too was terribly disappointed. Whatever mask of bravery I had on must have collapsed in a flash and for a moment he looked at me queerly. There was instant recognition of the plight.

"I like the variety," he said and quickly got on to another subject.

He had, I imagined, been sufficiently savaged in his own career to know how wounding criticism can be and that the most wounding of all was from those we respect and love. Most of us survive these periods and the redeeming aspect of the newspaper game is that everyone has a chance to rewrite his fortunes with a new assignment. I stuck with the column until I thought I had got it right and then stuck with it for a year longer just to show IT that I wasn't departing from the assignment with my tail between my legs.

Over the years, I learned from the Master many lessons, of which the most important was that there is, by times, an art to letting things be and to studying first the *needs* of your neighbour rather than his *failings*.

JOHN BASSETT

Major John Bassett, BA. Chairman of Baton Broadcasting Inc. and former Publisher of the now defunct Toronto Telegram. Born 25 August 1915 in Ottawa, Ontario. Educated at Ashbury College (Ottawa), Bishop's College School (Lennoxville, P.Q.) and the University of Bishop's College. Served during the Second World War as a Major in the Seaforth Highlanders of Canada. After the war, he was defeated at two attempts to find a seat in the House of Commons. Had a long history as a journalist and senior management figure in Canadian newspapers in Sherbrooke, Montreal and Toronto. Presided over the demise of the Toronto Telegram in 1971. Grandfather of tennis ace Carling Bassett. Married twice, with four sons and two daughters. Progressive Conservative, Anglican, Royalist.

Among those who worked at the old Toronto *Telegram*, it has become something of a tedious cliché to report that it was all one joyous lark. The inconsistent corollary to these tales (usually rather beery) was that Big John was a big shit. In truth, I suppose he provided ample evidence to many of the veracity of the latter observation: crummy salaries, a cavalier attitude towards women, intemperate harangues, absurd editorial stances, etc., etc. One heard the latest atrocities each day at work, shortly after checking the reporters' mailbox. If now these tales are told with retrospective annoyance, I do not think my memory serves me wrong in recalling the very same stories initially reported in an atmosphere approaching reverence. Frankly I idolized him. He gave me my first break and first job in journalism, based on a delightful (if fraudulent) perception of my character, but it was the foot in the door I needed and the reason I got it seemed irrelevant.

Mr. Bassett was a member of the Toronto Badminton and

Racquet Club. Was? Is! Just ask the old tennis pro who was forbidden to ever hit him a lob in a paid-for game. My father is also a member and because of that, in my youth, I had "child of member" rights to play on the tennis and squash courts. At some point during an inglorious career at Upper Canada College, I found a system for cutting classes towards the end of two mornings in the week. I couldn't go home, obviously, so I snuck off to the B & R which was only a few blocks away at the corner of St. Clair Avenue West and Yonge Street. All the squash courts at that hour were unused and so I would get dressed in my whites and chase the stupid ball around the stupid court all by myself. The back wall of a squash court was a more responsive partner than the gold-leaf electroscope in the UCC physics lab ever was. I could get away with this unfettered use of the courts until the early lunch hour when the businessmen started arriving for their noontide grunt-and-groan. Often enough, it was Mr. Bassett and his partner who politely threw me off the court. After a sufficient number of such encounters, he got it into his head that I was a very determined young fellow who was perfecting my squash skills with single-minded tenacity. I don't believe he ever wondered how it was I came to be there during school hours. No matter. When I turned 16, I asked him for a summer job and he arranged for my entry into journalism through the noble and time-honoured position of copyboy.

The *Tely* then was still located on Melinda Street and the chief of copyboys was a not entirely affectionate creature who had been Major Bassett's batman during the Second World War. The joint was crawling with Bassett cronies or friends of friends and sons of friends and even daughters of mistr . . . no, I'll not repeat the gossip. One got the impression the old man could never say no, but in fact he had a real gift for spurring someone on in their humble task with the wink of an eye or a hearty, bone-shattering slap on the back. He must have because the pay really was lousy — the worst of the three Toronto papers — yet people actually liked working there.

To me, he was always larger than life. My earliest memories of him were of a sort of John O'Hara character whose internal, psychological dynamics were kept rigorously secluded behind a barrage of amiable bluster and hearty camaraderie. When he walked through the newsroom and stopped at a reporter's desk for a few words, the journalist — male or female — was invariably reduced to jelly and was good for over-production for at least three weeks at $47 per.

Once, just after he had showered at the B&R, the foreign editor of the *Tely* called him and he picked up the telephone extension in the locker room standing stark naked. There were over a dozen people hanging around, talking the usual harmless banalities, when his loud voice forced us all to stop and listen.

"He's going to get the interview, eh? That's great. Play it up nicely. Make sure you tell him to tell Castro that he's hurting his nice image with all those executions. We think it's great Batista is gone, but he's won the day now and let's get on with improving Cuba. We sure don't want the Commies to get a toe-hold there."

This image of a newspaper publisher ranting off his instructions to a far-away correspondent has remained with me ever since. It is emblematic of some of the absurdities of the business and also much of its romance. For John Bassett was a romantic in life — and still is I assume. He loved being a publisher for the same reason a journalist loves being a journalist: because things happen, because one never knows what to expect, and because (however peripherally) one has a chance to intrude upon events as they happen and set them down. To be a witness, to be paid to be a witness, is wonderful. Take my word for it. A world of action, it is true, breeds a yearning for its opposite pole and many journalists are often overcome by a profound desire to get off their fast trains for the world of contemplation, which seems all the more alluring when the pace of events threaten to explode. But at its heart's core, alone with your eyes and your wits, action confronts you with the world as it is at the moment, and it is a pure and awesome to behold and be a part of.

And Action, albeit at a somewhat less sublime level, was what the ridiculous old *Tely* was all about. There was Action Line, of course, with Everyman's fearless ombudsman, Frank Drea, drifting out of the newsroom in an utter fog most nights. After rescuing Mrs. K of Scarborough from the clutches of her inaccurate vacuum cleaner guarantee, and admonishing G.R.K. of Perkins Carpets for the crummy shag he sold dear old Miss L of Alcina Avenue, Frank the Fearless had exhausted his daily capacity for compassion and left the premises to ride the fearful night, which variously appeared, in the fog, as a shadow monster or paper tiger. In the morning though, by God, he was always sober and snarling brightly once again.

When I finished graduate work in England, and none of the Toronto papers — save Big John's — would have me, I entered the vortex of the *Tely* on the overnight police desk, a charming post I loyally served for several months until, of all things, the music critic's post came free. My request for that job, submitted on a dare, was granted with no one more surprised than myself. The reason for this amazing foresight in assigning one so young to such an important post only became evident six months later when the paper folded: the powers that be were prepared to put *anyone* into the job just to fill it. I wasn't even told until a week later that it included ballet coverage, about which I knew sweet nothing. Thus are critics born, or used to be. Do not express shock: you suspected it all along. Vile and tawdry profession!

My colleagues-in-arms (a dangerous phrase at the *Tely*, I suppose) appear mythical to me now. Drea, for example, was nicknamed Dr. Death among the younger sports. His health seemed atrocious and it amazed us that he staggered through each week without ending up in the obituary column. In the end, he fought valiantly against his various demons and won, and his instinct for attack was usefully deployed by Premier William Davis when the *Tely's* own Don Quixote joined the Ontario provincial government.

Where on earth today could you go to find a crowd like the old gang at the *Tely*. To one's right was the poor man's Evelyn Waugh, Mackenzie Porter. Just across the way, Peter Worthington's blazing eyes glared out in Rasputin-like rage at nothing in particular. The drama critic, duBarry Campeau, her wig slightly askew and her billowing caftan snagged in a pencil sharpener, beckoned sweetly for someone — *anyone* — to help her out of this "perfectly dreadful predicament, I mean who needs pencils anyway?" Of the mad photographers, perhaps little should be said. Whenever I was allowed to join their lunatic assignments, I understood what combat in Vietnam must have been like. The row of junior editors, each trying to stab each other in the back and all succeeding, formed the summit of hierarchy for the most junior of reporters. Their numbers included Tim Porter, the son of Mackenzie and right now I see me approaching him in high rage, grasping his stupid assignment notice in my hand. It says: "Have booked photog. for 10:30 p.m. Wednesday. Go with him to Holbrook Estates for the Saturday real-estate front. Porter."

No bloody way, buddy. Everyone knows what the real-estate front is all about at the *Tely*. It's *corrupt*, that's what. If you buy a big enough ad, you can get a nice frothy puff-piece written by "one of our very own staff" and your tacky little houses will take off. Having struggled to get on dayshift for two months, this appeared to be the price: interview a g-d public relations goon for a construction or real-estate firm. No bloody way! I am John A. Fraser, M.A. I have read the metaphysical poets. I understand Lear's secret. I am moved by Johann Sebastian Bach and am not unmindful of Karlheinz Stockhausen. Hazlitt is my inspiration and Orwell my guide. Like Glendower, I can summon spirits from the lofty deep and for me they come when I call because I know the contemporary incantation: Frye and Frazer, Frazer and Frye (and if you don't understand that, then you Madam and you Sir are more worthy of trotting out to Holbrook Estates than I, whose Bachelor of Arts has Honours attached).

I declined the assignment, not giving the above reasons perhaps, but certainly suggesting their essence. Tim looked up at me with a look of one who had just learned that jerks were not only set above one's station in life, but also below.

"Why don't you just be professional instead of a horse's ass?" he said with a forced, cruel smile. "There's not an assignment you'll ever receive that can't be handled professionally. Unless of course you prefer to be a prima donna, in which case I'm sure I'm not worthy enough to handle your copy."

Here was a good lesson, learned in the nick of time. With a few suggestions, I started to clue in and went to the happy Holbrook Estates with excited anticipation. I heard out the flacks and patiently walked through their tacky model home. Then, after bidding adieu, I went around to 20 houses in the development that were already occupied and asked the owners what life was like in paradise. It turned out they had complaints: unfinished work, shoddy work, already disintegrating work, overpriced work. With my faithful Underwood, I looked down on Holbrook Estates with Zeus-like omnipotence. The feckless mythologists in the model house were contrasted with the honest burghers in the "architect designed" shanties. Non-existent services were fully depicted, as was the public transport, which hadn't even reached the planning stages for that area. Cracks in ceilings were lovingly accentuated and exposed live wires in basements crackled with pejorative adjectives. I handed it in, but had no feedback. On Saturday, the real-estate front featured only a picture display with an extended cutline that talked about "a price that will bring a smile to the first-time buyer." I was never again asked to do a real-estate story. I had been professional.

Not so Billington, the zany Entertainment Editor. He seemed six-foot-seven as he stomped around our refuse bin of a department in his ridiculous cowboy boots. He was quite wonderful, especially when he decided that God had personally chosen him to be the H.L. Mencken *and* Dorothy Parker

(God can do this sort of thing) of Canada.

Half an hour before the final deadline, a deadline *he* was supposed to be enforcing, Billington was still hard at work on a review of a country-and-western concert he had assigned himself.

"Hey everyone," he shouted. "Listen to this. It's god-damned brilliant, that's what it is. Just listen . . ."

Dear duBarry looked up from her typewriter, although her fingers never stopped once: "Isn't he perfectly delightful? Such enthusiasm! If only we knew how to control it."

Sid Adilman rarely employed sarcasm. "Knock it off David. We've all got stories to write."

"Hey, now listen man, I wouldn't do this if it wasn't terrific." Billington was remorseless, invincible, unstoppable. "*When she first walked into our midst, Kitty-Jean Kearney seemed a waif lost in the storm . . .*"

"DAVID. FOR CHRISSAKES. I haven't even managed to come up with a lead yet. Would you shut-up or I'll have to leave. You can't keep doing this all the time. You're supposed to be the editor."

Who said it? I can't remember. I think it was the late Bernadette Andrews, but I'm not sure. I just recall the sheer desperation.

"Well, hold on. Maybe listening to a really superb lead will help you. I'll start again: *When she first walked into our midst, Kitty-Jean Kearney seemed like a waif lost in the storm. But frailty was a mask and as her clear, cool voice lassoed the crowd at Cyclops' Tavern, we knew we were in the presence of strength and greatness.* Isn't that fantastic! Do you think 'lassoed' is pushing it a bit?"

"No," said duBarry. "You just leave that in. That's you."

"I think you're right," said Billington. "It's daring. A corny image in a fresh setting. It comes alive. That's what good C & W is all about."

"It just sings, dear," said duBarry. "Have you ever thought of showing these pieces to one of the newspapers? I'm sure there's an editor somewhere who will buy it."

We laughed. Billington told us to lay off and walked slowly back to the typewriter reading over his lead paragraph again, this time silently and just to himself. It was 15 minutes to deadline and he hadn't even prepared the lay-out pages. He was never late though. Not once. Within two years he won a National Newspaper Award for critical writing and the following year he won it again.

* * *

It was known she had been "seeing" the publisher. If you looked as good as she did, you'd be seeing the publisher too. But on this day, it is *High Noon* at *Search For Tomorrow*. As Isabel walks through the newsroom, everyone stops talking. Some of us pretend to type, but soon give up the charade. I think we all realize, more or less at the same time, that *she doesn't know*. But she must know. No, she couldn't know. She looks mystified and can't understand the charged atmosphere in the transformed newsroom. She hasn't seen that just about every desk around her has a copy of the *Globe and Mail* opened to the legal notices from Osgoode Hall. She has been named co-respondent in divorce proceedings by Mrs. John Bassett. Only George Anthony has the courage to go to her desk and tell her and then . . . and then . . . oh NO. The eyes are glistening. Those are real tears. Grown men weaken, grown women long to turn the page. George consoles her. What on earth are we all going to do? Who's writing the script here? We want to change the channel. The tension is getting out of hand.

From the back of the newsroom, a big man strides in.

"ISABEL," he shouts. Loudly, firmly, compassionately.

"I'm here John," she says, looking up and then standing.

He makes a hesitant step or two forward.

Turn the page, turn the page.

She takes a very deep breath and brushes a tear away with the back of one hand. She is very, very beautiful.

Turn the page, turn the page.

In slow motion they seem to glide towards each other. He puts his big arms around her and walks her out of the newsroom forever and off to the publisher's office.

Us guys? What do we do? We . . . applaud. I mean really! Who needs a raise when you can have a scene like that before the morning news conference has even been called?

* * *

Eighteen years later, he came to England with Isabel to see his granddaughter, Carling, play at Wimbledon. His fourth son, Matthew, is nearly half the age of the granddaughter. I swear he doesn't seem any older. Isabel and he continue to dazzle each other and his enthusiasm, if anything, is even stronger than it seemed two decades ago. He is still a commander of men, but Isabel has taught him about women's rights and those who didn't think the old boy could adjust didn't know him. He is much more open to the mysteries and wonder of life than he used to be. Not all us sinners get a second chance, but like Old Jolyn Forsyte in the Galsworthy saga, John Basset's Indian Summer stretches on and on.

He is still difficult to be around on the tennis court. Anyone who loathes losing the way he does is unpleasant to be around when he loses. At North Hatley, Quebec, where he used to have a famous summer home, the local Anglican Church had to change the hour of Holy Communion because the congregation always watched Big John take on his three boys at the local court on Sunday mornings. The histrionics were horrible but riveting; the language appalling, but minutely recorded. If this was paternal affection, what was fatherly annoyance like?

In London, 25 years later, his eldest son, Johnny F, his pride, is the occasion for summoning up a rough-hewn, pure affection. But the stricken heir is far away and very sick, and he, Big John Bassett, is in the end a humble supplicant before unfathomable irony. He knows enough to be in awe of fate and he is in touch with his best emotions. And here the page can rest.

J. TUZO WILSON

John Tuzo Wilson, CC, OBE, PhD, DSc, FRCS, FRS. Geophysicist, educator, author. Born 24 October 1908 in Ottawa, Ontario. Educated at the University of Toronto, Cambridge University and Princeton University. Eighteen honorary degrees from various universities around the world; member of 11 Canadian and foreign scientific academies; past president or chairman of four international scientific associations; honorary fellow of six universities or colleges; winner of at least 16 international and Canadian medals for significant scientific achievements. He has led a colourful and varied life which is nevertheless rooted in brilliant, original work studying the plate tectonic phenomenon in continental drift. Not content with pure research, he has been an innovative educator and has travelled the world to share his knowledge. He has a significant reputation in the People's Republic of China as a "scientific friend of the Chinese people", which is second only to Dr. Joseph Needham of Great Britain. During his youth he spent many summers in geological research and made the first ascent of Mt. Hague in Montana (12,328 feet) in 1938. Served in the Second World War and rose to the rank of Lieutenant-Colonel at Canadian Military Headquarters Overseas (1942-43) and Colonel and Director of Operational Research at National Defence Headquarters (1943-46). After the war, he devoted himself to further research and education. Among his notable positions in Canada, he was Professor of Geophysics at the University of Toronto (1946-74) and Principal of the University of Toronto's new Erindale College (1967-74). Upon retirement from active academic life, he was appointed Director General of the Ontario Science Centre where he remained for 11 years. He is currently Chancellor of York University. Married, with two daughters.

Although he is married to a close relative of my wife's, I have always been a trifle shy in the presence of Professor

Wilson. No doubt, this has something to do with my presiding ignorance about science in any of its forms. He is also an achiever of such stature that I never thought anything I could think of to say would have much relevance in his life.

His peers may revere him for his pioneering work in geophysics and the Ontario public may be grateful that at the end of his professional career he chose to head up the famous Science Centre in Toronto, which helps ignoramuses like me come to terms with unseen forces, but I shall always be grateful that he installed a humus toilet at his cottage at Go Home Bay.

"Wonderful invention," he said with matter-of-fact pleasure. "It's the answer to pollution and it's been there all along. The Chinese have been recycling human waste for thousands of years and we're just catching up."

I can't say I liked the experience of sitting on a humus toilet. It hums and vibrates a lot, which may aid digestion but does nothing for your sense of confidence in a precarious and exposed situation. The combination of the rather warm seat and the ominous sounds suggests one is on some sort of projectile in the final stages of countdown.

Still, everyone worries about "wastes" in Georgian Bay. Septic tanks are disgusting and inefficient. Retaining tanks are even more disgusting. Getting a vast tile bed for a proper flusher costs as much as the building of the Petit Trianon at Versailles. Thus the logic of a humus toilet which breaks down "wastes" into tidy bundles of odour-acceptable fertilizer.

The system does have its eccentricities, some of which need not be described here. One which can, however, is the necessity to "feed" the beast with vegetable matter: dried moss, potato peelings, pea pods and heaven knows what else. The idea is that after the appropriate duration, the genial proprietor of the humus toilet just takes out his perfectly-packaged fertilizer and disposes of it in an environmentally sound way —on a vegetable garden or on the front lawn back home in Toronto.

The following summer, I went to tea at the Wilsons and

inquired after the humus toilet.

"Stupid thing isn't worth a damn," said Professor Wilson.

"What's gone wrong?" I asked incredulously.

"Don't know. But it's not doing what it is supposed to do. I had to dig out all the muck and cart it back into the woods. Horrible job."

He shivered in disgust at the memory.

I went back home, pulled out *Who's Who* and reread his entry; the third longest in a 1250-page tome. There it was: 18 honorary degrees, fellowships in all the most notable scientific institutes in the world, medals and awards from dozens of important organizations, books and pamphlets giving evidence of a diverse and inquiring intelligence. But there's a little spot waiting for the terrible truth. It can be placed somewhere between the item "made first ascent of Mt. Hague, Montana (12,328 feet) in 1935" and "the Penrose Medal, Geol. Society America" and it will read: "Defeated by humus toilet, Go Home Bay, 1984."

DONALD JAMIESON

Honourable Donald Jamieson, PC. Retired broadcaster, politician and statesman. Born 30 April 1921 in St. John's, Newfoundland. Educated at Prince of Wales College in St. John's. A self-made millionaire who literally started from the bottom (bellhop at the old Newfoundland Hotel), he parlayed a gift for the gab into a small broadcasting empire which he ran jointly with his brother, Colin Jamieson. Was first elected to the House of Commons in 1966 and got his first cabinet post (Defense Production) two years later. One of the big names in successive Trudeau administrations, he served variously as Minister of Transport, Minister of Regional Economic Expansion, Minister of Industry Trade and Commerce, and finally Minister of External Affairs. He resigned his federal seat to lead the Newfoundland Liberal Party in 1979 and was briefly Leader of the Opposition. From 1982 to 1985, he was High Commissioners to the United Kingdom. Married, with three daughters and one son. Presbyterian.

T hey were all gathered round the bar at Marty's pub, opposite the War Memorial, on Duckworth Street in St. John's. The lashing rain outside seemed to contribute mightily to the conviviality and comradeship of those inside. High up on the wall, a television set was placed on a wobbly perch and the bartender was flicking a series of switches trying to find the horizontal hold.

"Yes, b'y. Dat's got it. Dat's Don. Just leave it be now."

Welcome to CJON-TV's coverage of the Newfoundland provincial election, circa 1966. We are now several hours before the first ballots are to be counted, but in order to size up the situation, cut the political cloth to order, test out the waters, read the barometer and get a feel for the big vote, CJON is featuring its proprietor and chief on-air personality for two hours and 17 minutes of non-stop commentary. As a public service, there won't even be commercials.

"Some good, ain't 'e?" said the old trout at the bar as he nodded approvingly at the flickering image of Don Jamieson on the screen. "Dey jess sets 'im hinfront of dat TV camera and de talking comes and comes. 'E can keep dat hup fer 'ours, 'e can. I jess loves listenin' to 'im."

In truth, he was a marvel and he did keep it up for hours. Little-known facts from Burgeo, an unattended statistic from Joe Batt's Arm, a warm anecdote from Fogo, a nod in the direction of Miss Conception Bay who may well have hailed from Dildo, precedents established by the old Dominion of Newfoundland government of Sir Richard Squires, memories of the Honourable Joseph R. Smallwood from his earlier days, memorable visitors to Gander International Airport — all were grist to Don's mill and leavened his metaphors until they shone like mixed jujubes in a concoction whose beginning and ending were wholly peripheral to his unfettered ability to keep the words coming and coming so that the sentences meshed without seams into paragraphs that were veritable skyscrapers set against a political landscape where you really could see the trees for the forest and grown men shivered at the wonder of it all, for such was his gift of the gab.

This was also Newfoundland's gift to Ottawa and Ottawa's gift to the cause of world peace. For those of us who knew the Honourable Don by his words alone, there was no doubt whatsoever that as long as he could be present (as Secretary of State for External Affairs) at the councils of world ministers and be allowed a fair say in their affairs, there would be no war. Not only would no one know when to begin a conflagration, by the time he might reach his peroration no one would remember why a possible war might be started in the first place.

I never knew him personally in St. John's or in Ottawa, although for a lark I sometimes listened in to the simultaneous translations in French during House of Commons debates or committee hearings: occasionally a dazed interpreter would go off the deep end after getting lost in the luxuriant imagery and back-ended syntax. You could tell the interpreter was in trouble because he was translating Don's English into English and still struggling to find the right words. Once, during an important trip he made to the People's Republic of China, a rather long-winded but extremely courteous paragraph (sky-scraper variety) expressing his delight in being in China was translated thusly:

"The honourable minister said he was happy to be in China. He said it four times in four different ways."

I did get to know him in London and to my utter amazement not only got along with him reasonably well, but grew very fond of his bluster and came to admire his kindness which was bestowed on anyone — high or low — who would share a laugh or a cigarette with him.

During the Christmas and New Year season in London, it was the custom of this particular High Commissioner to invite a sizeable number of the resident Canadian community in Britain to dine at his residence. These were hearty, Pickwick-ian affairs in which the host, full of the prevailing spirit, let all the formalities down and presided over Yuletide feasts notable for their down-home vitality. I missed the 1984 occasion, but I sure heard about it when I got back to town.

My colleague P had already arranged to have his parents over from Canada for Christmas in England when the Honour-able Don sent him an invitation for the big "do" at the High Commission. When a discreet inquiry was put out to see if the parents could be included in the gathering, the answer came back immediately: of course. And so, P's mother and father came to the glittering affair. For his mother particularly, it was a very big event as she had never before been in such surround-ings or in such august company. She was proud of her son, proud of her country, proud of England, proud of Christmas and New Year's, proud of just about anything. Perhaps sensing this, and maybe also a bit of unease, the High Commissioner

181

placed her at his own table. Now this is quite typical of him and part of his general admirableness, even when he went a little awry in his conversation, which was also typical of him.

After sketching aspects of his life in London with the big bankers, the landed gentry, the aristocracy, indeed even with the Royal Family, the Honourable Don got a bit of a twinkle in his eyes as he turned to his table companions and said:

"But you know, at the end of the day, nothing with those VIPs counts as much as being able to snuggle your nose between your wife's snowy breasts."

The image appealed to him so much, he repeated it. As I said to P, it wasn't what I would have said if I were High Commissioner, but then Mr. Trudeau didn't send me, did he? And no one can ever call Don Jamieson a phoney. Every air he ever put on, he always went overboard to undermine (I deploy one of his own expressions and a rather powerful one at that).

The Queen, I am able to report, also appreciated the Honourable Don's anecdotes (which really were wonderful, mostly) and his shameless but never unwelcome flattery. I do not have this on hearsay, I have it as a direct witness. At the Commonwealth Day reception at Marlborough House, Queen Mary's former royal residence in London, I was chatting amiably to the High Commissioner as Her Majesty was slowly making her way out the front hall through a thick crowd.

We were standing in the crowd two back from the front line where people were crowding to get a closer look at the Queen, and, I believe, we were talking about Brian Peckford's chances in the next provincial election in Newfoundland. The next thing I knew, the flow of my words was cut off mid-stream (I share certain traits with the High Commissioner, like garru- lousness and metaphor mongering) and the people in front of us parted to reveal a gloved hand stretched out in the direction of the Honourable Don:

"Mr. High Commissioner," said the unmistakable voice, "I thought that was you hiding out back there."

He bent over and kissed her hand. He is not a slight man, the

Honourable Don, and the bending could not have been easy, but there was dignity and genuinely touching drama in the encounter. The Queen clearly liked him and liked him in the right way, because her face betrayed both a desire to chuckle at a still-unheard anecdote and a warmth felt towards this one plenipotentiary who, while he knew his place, never bored her with formal awe.

They talked for a few minutes, but you will not find me betraying a Royal Conversation. Suffice it to say, Her Majesty knew her man and he knew what was expected of him. Her laughter is rarely heard in public, but it is quite becoming and wholly unforced. I would not say she was actually flirting with a courtier, for that would be unseemly reportage and possibly disloyal. I will note however, without comment, that it was only towards the very end of her conversation that she remembered to inquire after his wife.

HERBERT WHITTAKER

Herbert Whittaker, OC. Drama critic emeritus of Canada. Born September 20, 1910 in Montreal, Quebec. Educated at Strathcona Academy and Ecole des Beaux Arts in Montreal. Initially an arts writer at the Montreal Gazette, *he was drama critic at the Toronto* Globe and Mail *from 1949 to 1975, during which time he was also critic for just about every other performing arts category until the paper gradually developed a proper arts section. Throughout the years, he has directed, designed and adjudicated plays across Canada and is the author of several books and the recipient of numerous awards. He has served on the boards of leading Canadian theatrical and perform-ing arts institutions, including the National Theatre School in Mont-real, the National Arts Centre in Ottawa and the Stratford Shakespea-rean Festival. He is the first lifetime member of the Canadian Actors Equity Association. Unmarried.*

It was always said of Herbie's theatre reviews in the *Globe and Mail* that if you knew his code words and special signals, it was possible to get a perfect fix on the offering at hand. Thus, if he began a review commending "the helpful lighting scheme" of such-and-such a technical director, you knew right from the onset that the production was a turkey. Although he had and continues to have several legions of admirers across the land and around the world, it is also true that his nurturing approach to criticism irritated others, both inside and outside the theatre. The legendry rivalry with Nathan Cohen at the Toronto *Star* is thought by some scholars of Canadian theatre to be the very definition of the two major schools of criticism in the land: the one hectoring or wildly expansive, the other — Herbie's — quietly encouraging or gently chiding.

As a result, many people who do not know the man came to

the false concluson that he always declined to strike out at the things he disliked and that he lacked tenacity of viewpoint. Nothing could be further from the truth. His off-the-page analysis of new productions was often withering in the extreme and deadly accurate. Occasionally, and he always regretted it later, his annoyance would emerge in print with devastating effect. Toronto Free Theatre, for example, once put on one of its shock-horrors which featured the usual nudity and outrageous sexual harangues. I can't remember the play's name, just Herbie's review. A swashbuckling young Toronto male lead, who shall remain nameless, turned out to be the lightning rod for the critic's ire. "There's no difficulty locating this actor on the crowded stage," wrote Herbie in his review. "He's the one with the tiny penis."

A few weeks later, I heard from Martin Kinch, artistic director of the troupe, what happened after the review appeared. The actor, not surprisingly, was outraged — which I assume Herbie fully intended. Like the judges at Nuremberg, he did not believe underlings should blindly follow the orders of their superiors: actors were no less exempt from culpability in nefarious deeds than were ordinary well-intentioned Germans. The actor had a mind to go on the legal warpath and sue both Herbie and the newspaper.

"That's going to be interesting," observed the wry Mr. Kinch as he tried to calm the actor. "What are you going to do? Take it out in a court of law and ask the jury for a decision? Are you sure you are up to that?"

The legal suit remained flaccid.

The charge of lacking a viewpoint is easily refuted. Herbie's whole life has been given over to a devotion to the stage and its people — that is his viewpoint. Few people have been more consistent for so long a time, and such has been his faithfulness, that it has borne him through all vicissitudes and controversies. His inner certainty and tranquility about the true nature of his only mistress allowed him to pass off the mundane chores and irritations of daily life with a clever quip or a degree of sweet illogic that was sometimes awesome to behold.

Some of his lines I will cherish till the day I die. Once, for example, we were all back at our desks late at night writing furiously for our edition deadline. The Night Entertainment Editor was in a foul mood and was clearly cruising for an outbursts to release his bile. All of us, save Herbie, recognized the tell-tale signs and worked hard to keep out of J's line of fire.

The venerable theatre critic, however, trotted amiably out of his office with the first page of his review. I assume this copy was no different in substance and style from what he normally produced, and which I myself had edited from time to time as the back-up "late-trick" editor in the department. That meant the usual assortment of mis-spellings and baroque grammatical construction. It also meant margins stretched to both edges of the page and lines spaced only sufficiently wide to allow Herbie's own extensive handwritten additions to the typed text. Sometimes these additions would go travelling all over the place, meandering down the thin margin on the right and gathering in a chunky clump at the bottom of the page with seemingly aimless arrows pointing out in opposite directions as a guide to the hapless editor.

After handing in the first page of his copy, Herbie went contentedly back to his office to write the second. A minute later J exploded with nuclear vigour. Here I have to reconstruct part of the harangue which ensued because the particular point of irritation eludes me all these years after the event. Let's say Herbie mis-spelled Shakespeare's name. He did it often enough (so did Shakespeare, but that's another point). J leapt up from his chair and literally started hopping up and down on the spot, banging the desk with his fist all the while.

"You're supposed to be the most experienced goddamned theatre critic in the whole goddamned country and you can't even spell the name of the most important fucking playwright in the English language. How the hell can you look at yourself in the mirror? How the . . ."

Everyone around J stopped writing, but kept their eyes glued to their typewriters. Across the vast expanse of the mostly empty newsroom, a copyboy peered over our way to see if someone had died. At first Herbie remained an unseen presence hidden away in his office and then we were aware that he had emerged and was walking softly towards the raging beast at the copy desk.

He stood in front of J with a quiet and wholly unbelligerent smile on his face and finally the harangue simply stopped:

"Why J," said Herbie with ominous restraint, "I put those little errors in there so that you can feel you have a function in life. I thought you'd be grateful."

I have myself been able to employ that line from time to time and am happy here to acknowledge its true author. I was less happy when the old Editor-in-Chief ordered me one day to assist Herbie out of his expense account problem following an extensive tour of East Europe, of which the highlight was the wondrous welcome he got in Poland after the indifferent and sometimes surly reception in the Soviet Union.

"Look, you've got to help me with the accounts department," said The Boss one day. "Herbie is now seven months overdue on handing in his expenses for that trip and they're phoning me every other day. I want you to sit down with him and account for the $1,800 he spent. And I want it done as soon as possible."

I was immediately fussed about hurting Herbie's feelings. I'd only been at the *Globe* for two years and he had been there since time began. He was then, and remains, my kindest mentor.

"Herbie," I said when I called him at home, "they've asked me to help you get this expense account in. They've been waiting a long time and think you may be having a problem with the forms. If you don't want anything to do with the idea, it's okay with me. We can both tell them to stuff it."

"Not want you to help! Dear boy, you've come on an errand of mercy and salvation. When can we do it?"

Easier said than done.

When we finally sat down, I soon realized he didn't have one receipt for the entire four-week trip, except for his airline ticket which had been purchased for him by the office and for which he didn't have to account.

"But didn't you ask for receipts?" I asked in wonderment. I am one who had been trained by the very best in the business not to sneeze on the job without a receipt.

"Certainly not," said Herbie with the disdain of a High Edwardian for the sleazy paraphernalia of cash transactions. "Someone would ask me for money and I would give it to them. It all worked out very well."

"Alright," I said as I began to measure up manfully to the true dimension of the task that lay ahead, "let's go about this in a business-like way."

"Oh let's not," said Herbie. "How about a glass of sherry?"

"No. I want you to get your diary for that trip and we're going to go through what you did, day by day."

"What fun. I haven't been able to get anyone to listen to the whole adventure. It may be useful to you."

In fact it was a hoot of an account and I should have had a tape-recorder going. His insights into the dilemma facing any creative artist under the dictatorship of the proletariat were the best primer I ever had before I went to China five years later, while his faith in people who toil on the stage under whatever conditions taught me to be wary of ostensibly observable facts.

While he talked on, I made careful note of how many days he spent in Moscow or Warsaw or wherever and noted under each date and place little headings like Hotel, Meals, Taxis, Entertainment, Supplies, and that beloved catch-all — Miscellaneous. With a pocket calculator, I divided the $1,800 by the appropriate number of days and further divided the days into the heading categories. I was a whiz. Herbie watched my fingers fly on the little digits with the fascination of a Borneo native looking at his first Polaroid camera.

"Isn't that a wonderful little machine. I must get one. Will you teach me how to use it?" he asked.

"No," I said firmly. "It would be counter-productive."

I was one possessed by the task at hand at this juncture. Page after page of expense account forms noted an expensive taxi foray in Gdansk, a reciprocal dinner for hosts in Leningrad, newspapers in Moscow (no matter that Herbie didn't read Russian, it was a legitimate expense — even a sacred one) and room service in Prague. I carefully noted after most entries that the relevant authorities had declined to offer receipts and made xerox copies of obscure pages in the theatre programs Herbie collected which I was sure would fool the accounts department. If questioned, I would simply say I had included them as proof of passage. To these I affixed the airline ticket voucher and stuck them all into what became a pleasingly thick envelope marked "Receipts and Attachments".

The actual expense account, when completed, was a work of beauty. I was almost convinced he had actually done things the way I had itemized them.

"Have a look at that," I said with justifiable pride, "and when you finish reading it, sign at the bottom of each page."

He took the pages from me like Wagner must have received his librettist's lines: in anticipation, trepidation and gratitude. I didn't expect him to understand any of it, merely admire the neat entries and my skill as a writer of plausible fiction. I was a trifle annoyed to see him furrow his brow on the third page and then flip back to the first.

"What's the matter?" I asked.

"Well I'm not signing this and that's flat," he said.

"What do you mean? Why on earth not?"

"Well," Herbie said in some agitation, "you have the Poles charging me more money than the Russians. That won't do at all."

"For heaven's sake, Herbie. You spent much longer in Poland than in the Soviet Union. Obviously you spent more money there."

"You're forgetting one thing, aren't you? You're forgetting the Poles treated me very decently indeed. I didn't care for the Russians at all."

"Honest to God, I don't believe this is happening. Will you just sit down there and sign these accounts please?"

"I'll sign it if you insist, but I'll have to make a note beside my signature that I am signing in protest and that these figures do not actually represent the trip as I experienced it."

"Sweet Mary and Joseph! Here, give me that stupid thing. You're not going to write anything but your name at the bottom."

I snatched back the expense account and where it had said USSR I wrote in Poland on top of white-out typing correction fluid. Where it said Poland, I wrote USSR. I left the geographically impossible stopping-off points alone, figuring — correctly as it turned out — that the powers-that-be would be so grateful for anything even approximating an expense account that they would approve it without demur.

"That's much better'" said Herbie who inscribed his formal signature with the dignity of a governor general passing a bill of law.

"You'll get a refund of nearly $25 from the company. The first commandment of expense accounts is *never* have the sum total equal the advance funds. The second is like unto it: never have them come in under the advance funds, always over. On these two commandments hang all the Law and the Profits.

"Well," said Herbie, amused at the sacrilege, "that's only fitting. These trips are very expensive. I don't know if I can do too many more."

"What's that to you?" I asked, not understanding his point at all. "The paper pays for everything."

"Yes, yes, it is very generous, but I ran out of its money before I got out of Poland."

"For heaven's sake, all they gave you was an advance. If you spend more, you claim for it in the expense account. That's what expense accounts are for. How much of your own money

190

did you spend?"

"None of your business. It was a great privilege to get that trip. I'll always be grateful, just as I'm grateful to you for helping me out of this silly problem."

Sic transit Herbie.

HUGH MacLENNAN

Hugh MacLennan, CC, MA, PhD. Novelist and educator. Born in Glace Bay, Nova Scotia on March 20, 1907. Educated at the Halifax Academy, Dalhousie University, Oxford University (Rhodes Scholar) and Princeton University. Author of numerous books of which some of the most famous include Barometer Rising *(1941),* Two Solitudes *(1945),* Each Man's Son *(1951) and* The Watch That Ends the Night *(1959 Winner of the Governor General's Award for Fiction). Numerous honorary degrees, awards and literary medals. Professor Emeritus at McGill University where he taught for several decades. Married twice. No children.*

I t was late afternoon in North Hatley, Quebec. On a grassy bank overlooking Lake Massawippi (which, I still hold, was named by an Indian with a lisp), the staff of Hovey Manor were trotting out the tea trays. MacCallum (the wife) and I had come down to see the offerings of the Lennoxville Festival, which I was required to review as the *Globe and Mail's* new theatre critic. As usual, I had a secondary purpose, as it had been nearly 15 years since I had worked in nearby Sherbrooke in the first reporting job I landed at the *Record*. Nostalgia is a terrible failing in one so young, but I have been a victim of it since the age of 12 and there is no cure.

As we lay in the deck chairs, munching the cucumber sandwiches and guzzling Earl Grey, a voice that could have been confused with the Cape Race foghorn boomed out from a neighbouring table:

"Well, Sybil. I don't care what they say about these Frenchies. That was a very tolerable driver we had."

The voice's companion launched into the local argot:

"Wasn't he just! *Très bien habillé, si vous savez.*"

MacCallum propped her head up a bit and her eyes widened, then rolled wildly in my direction.

"I know who the old girl is," I hissed with delight. "It's Mrs. M and that must be her 'niece,' the dreaded Miss P."

I'd never met Mrs. M, but I knew mountains of guff about her. Formidable. Indomitable. Well into her eighties, she had once been seen hooking a slowly moving taxicab with her walking stick and bringing it to a full halt on Avenue Road near her home in Toronto.

"Well, let's keep well clear," said the ever-sensible spouse.

"Sure," I said. "We don't want to mess around in that league."

Poor MacCallum. We had hardly been married a year and she still hadn't fully discovered what she was saddled with.

We gathered our things and made our way back to the main lodge of Hovey Manor. MacCallum took a wide arc away from Mrs. M, but I headed straight for her.

"Are you Mrs. M?" I demanded.

"Why, yes I am," said the booming voice. "Who the devil are you?"

"I'm John Fraser and I think we have some mutual acquaintances. Down to see the theatre are you?"

Out of the corner of my eye I could see MacCallum looking on in disbelief. Well, well. A journalist can't get ahead without the widest possible contacts. After a bit more aimless banter, I saluted the ladies and rejoined Apoplexy Personified.

"I don't believe you just did what you did," she said.

We were laughing when we got into the bedroom, but the moment I entered the room I realized our southern window looked out directly over Mrs. M, whose voice echoed throughout the interior.

"Close the window," said MacCallum.

"What do you mean? This could be fun."

There was a little lull in the conversation. Wife and husband were on their knees on top of the bay window banquette to hear as clearly as possible the pearls of wisdom from below.

Mrs. M didn't disappoint.

"So that's John Fraser. Seemed nice enough. Still, he's a bit fatter than I thought he'd be."

The thrill of self-recognition was only slightly marred by the evident amusement of my dear spouse. I feared her hoots of stifled laughter would reach the conversationalists. Her own moment, however, was not long in coming.

"The wife is supposed to be difficult. She moved in before they got married, you know. Terrible fuss."

Naturally, I warmed to Mrs. M thereafter. She was . . . how shall I put it? . . . unpredictable. Throughout the weekend we had numerous encounters. Her interests were varied and although she was the mistress of Received Opinion, her views were so regally contemptuous that I found myself smoking her out on any number of subjects. You must appreciate that MacCallum and I had brought down the average age of the residents of Hovey Manor by some 30 or 40 years. In the main lounge during the morning, ladies who frolicked as children during the reign of Victoria tatted and knitted with declining vigour. Over all the clicking, the unmistakable sounds could be heard of several emphysema victims gasping for breath. A clocked ticked. The woodwork creaked. Even discreetly whispered conversations brought furrows to ancient brows. It was in this setting one morning that Mrs. M boomed out the demand: "Well, Mr. Fraser, what d'ye make of Stratford this year?"

I tried to talk at a level of voice which was a compromise between hers and the sepulchral sounds surrounding. I said this about that production and that about this production, but Mrs. M was fidgety and clearly not all that interested in my view of theatrical aesthetics:

"Well, that's all very well, Mr. Fraser," she bellowed, "but I'm quite disturbed by all this homosexual perspective. Man did you see those outfits of the soldiers in *Antony and Cleopatra?* They looked like an army of poof boys."

The knitting and the tatting stopped dead. One of the ailing elderly clutched her breast as she gasped for extra air.

"I mean I have nothing against homosexuals, Mr. Fraser. Very talented, very talented. But it's not the only point of view."

Mrs. M said "homosexual" in a variant of the British pronounciation, with a short first "o" and a wee lisp on the "s". This way, it sounded like the most venal vice known to mankind.

"Well, I must go," said Mrs. M. "Please join Sybil and me for dinner tonight. Hugh MacLennan is coming and we'd enjoy your company.

MacCallum by this time had returned to her work in Toronto, but she would have been sorry to have missed the great novelist who, by this time, had entered into semi-mythology. I myself was quite keyed up by the prospect.

At the appointed hour, I joined the ladies on the lawn to await Mr. MacLennan. He was late and Mrs. M had the punctuality of royalty and wasn't amused. As we sipped our drinks, she facing out to the lake and I facing the manor's doorway, she offered few *pensées* on the still absent guest of honour.

"He's brilliant, of course. But they say he's gone a bit dotty . . ."

As she was shouting this out, the subject himself was emerging from the hall door and approaching our party. Mr. MacLennan was walking very slowly as he supported his wife who was clearly still ailing from some sort of leg injury. Even if one knew how to stop Mrs. M in mid-thought, it would have needed a braver man that I to attempt it. I felt frozen in horror and indecision.

". . . especially on the subject of the Kennedy assassination. He's got some bug about a conspiracy. So be warned. Whatever we do, no one must bring up the subject of the Kennedy assass . . ."

There was a smile on the novelist's face. A wonderful warm and broad smile, and I knew at once he felt as I did kneeling with MacCallum in the room above. It is an amusing and often pleasurable thing to be the source of controversy and gossip if you are actually lucky enough to hear it direct. In our lives, we receive or pass along so many pieces of worthless or inaccurate information about others that it is also medicinal, every now and then, to hear the same nonsense about our humble selves. humble selves.

"Ssshhh," said Mr. MacLennan in a voice loud enough to match Mrs. M's, "he's coming now."

"Oh thanks," said Mrs. M to the voice behind her, quite oblivious to its source. A few seconds later, the honoured guests were before their hostess.

"Mr. MacLennan, what an honour," said Mrs. M, and she truly meant it. "We were just saying how much we all enjoyed *The Watch That Ends The Night*. You have enriched all our lives."

"That I have ma'am," said Mr. MacLennan. "In many ways, I'm sure! What a pleasure to be here with you this evening and how kind of you to arrange it all . . ."

GINA MALLET

Gina Mallet. The mystery woman of the review columns. Former researcher with Time *magazine. Former drama critic of the Toronto Star. Whereabouts today:* inconnue.

During intermissions at opening nights, theatre critics gather together like witches at their cauldron. During one of the Stratford Festival openings — it was *Three Sisters* by Chekov directed by John Hirsch — Gina (Miss or Ms. Mallet seems somehow wrong) came up to me and started talking about the "superb" production value the audience was getting. This was at a time when Robin Phillips was still ruling the roost at Stratford, and Gina had been going after the British-born director with particular glee that season.

I tried to get off the subject of the play because it is always hard for me to come to my own conclusions if I have someone else's ideas ricocheting around in my late-night brain. But I shouldn't have worried. She was out stalking bigger game that night.

"What this bloody company needs is someone with *real* theatrical values like John Hirsch to run things . . . You know I think the police or the whitecoats are going to come for Robin any day."

What's this? What's this? Gina was stirring the cauldron with enthusiasm. I suppose her gift for dark gossip was genetic, but I liked to think she honed her skills working as a researcher for *Time* magazine in New York. I have a vision of that place filled with unusable file material gathered by eager little beavers like Gina. Black materials. The sort of stuff the FBI and CIA collect. The vision continues: I imagine *Time* editors, much in the style of J. Edgar Hoover, consulting their black files with the tut-tutting superiority of those who know the *real* truth but "are unable to reveal it at this time."

Gina's latest black materials on Robin Phillips produced a potent brew. At the end of intermission, the score was Hirsch 5 and Phillips -7. Since she herself made the rules, she was a convincing score-keeper.

Some years later, Gina was still loyally hacking away at theatre crits for the Toronto *Star*. When I saw her next, it was after a three year absence during which time I had been posted to China and had had some experience with the potency of other black file materials. I had been shocked, on my return, to learn that the lady was now out for the scalp of John Hirsch, who had succeeded Phillips as Stratford's artistic director. I was also shocked — nay staggered — when I saw a large piece Gina wrote in the *Star* eulogizing Phillips as a film director (he was then putting the finishing touches to *The Wars*, which turned out to be a box-office turkey).

When I finally ran across her again, during the intermission of a National Ballet of Canada performance at the O'Keefe Centre, I went about the always delicate process of smoking her out. It is delicate because you have to be careful not to be hit in the process: the lady's tongue would bring a blush to the cheek of a Restoration scoundrel. She has an alarming physical resemblance to Clive Barnes, the portly New York theatre and dance critic. Also, I believe she is incapable of talking gossip straightfaced. She is always looking over her shoulder as the terrible tales come pouring out, almost like a nervous dissident in a communist country being interviewed in a park.

"I was fascinated by your piece on Phillips," I said, not entirely innocently.

"Ah right," she responded. "Robin's really got his act together."

"And Hirsch?" I asked sweetly.

She looked conspiratorily behind her right shoulder. Then behind her left. She leaned forward and hissed:

"We've got him by the balls."

"Why?" I was playing the innocent sojourner, recently returned from far-away lands.

The black file was brought out and several items were dangled before my eyes. She even claimed to have information on his boyhood behaviour when he was cruelly incarcerated in a Nazi concentration camp. She finished up with the simple, but eloquent statement: "He's got to go."

"But who should replace him?"

"Anyone," said Gina.

The end-of-intermission warning bell had sounded. It was time to leave the world of reality for the realm of pure fantasy.

PETER NEWMAN

Peter Newman, OC, BA, MCOM. Journalist and author. Born in Vienna, Austria on May 10, 1929. Educated at local schools before emigrating to Canada where he went to Upper Canada College and the University of Toronto. Joined the Financial Post *in 1951. His first association with* Maclean's *Magazine was in 1956 as an assistant editor. In 1960 he became Ottawa Editor of the Toronto* Star *and remained at that newspaper for 11 years, acting succesively as National Affairs Editor, syndicated columnist and finally Editor-in-Chief. From 1971 to 1982 he was Editor-in-Chief of* Maclean's *and presided over the change to a weekly news magazine. The author of numerous books on politics and economics, he pioneered a new style of political reportage that is still the basis of most coverage coming out of Ottawa today. He is the recipient of numerous awards, medals and honorary degrees. Married twice, with one daughter.*

There are really quite a lot of curious stories about Peter Newman, which have been floating about for many years. Having never worked for or with him, I cannot personally testify to their authenticity, although life for me and countless other journalists would have been infinitely more dull had we never heard or been able to bandy them about.

I did, however, first encounter him under unusual circumstances in the late Sixties in Newfoundland and the man I met bore little resemblance to the spectral hero of all the tales I keep on hearing. He seemed to me then, and still does, a solemn and solitary figure who has somehow worked out a professional accommodation to loneliness and hugely profited thereby.

After he had written *Renegade In Power*, an epochal study of John Diefenbaker's loony years in power, which was the very first truly exciting political book ever written in Canada about Canadian politics, he found himself following Mr. Diefenbaker's tattered banner in St. John's during one of those indistinguishable election campaigns in the Sixties. Curiously, he was allowed to travel on the Diefenbaker campaign bus, but he always took a seat well to the rear and was treated, not surprisingly, as a pariah by the Chieftain's staff.

In those days, I lived in residence at Queen's (Anglican) College in St. John's, just around the corner from the old Newfoundland Hotel where Mr. and Mrs. Diefenbaker were put up for the most hopeless two days of his campaign. (Premier Smallwood, a Liberal, still decided who would represent Newfoundland in the House of Commons and, as far as I could determine, this included the occasional Tory.) I had the honour of shaking The Chief's hand as he emerged from the hotel one day as I was walking by.

"Mr. Diefenbaker!" I said in mock surprise, as I had been "walking by" for nearly 20 minutes waiting to bump into him. "May I shake your hand, Sir?"

There's a very silly impulse inside of me to seek out Pooh Bahs of any sort and press flesh with them. I try to control it now that I am in my fourth decade, not always successfully. I think it all stems from being given a horsey-ride on the knees of the Marquis of Milford Haven at the age of four. (His Grace, as I later learned, was bumming his way around North America, staying with friends of friends of friends, until he had located an heiress sufficiently well-endowed — I speak of finances only — to repair the family properties in Wales and London.) Hardly a day goes by without giving thanks to God Almighty for withholding both the means and the occasion to pursue this dreadful impulse in high places. As a further precaution, He has given me a wife who, if the means or occasion ever arise, will ensure that it is (mostly) eschewed.

Anyway, The Chief was good enough for my undergraduate days.

"Delighted young man, delighted." His jowls shook just as

Macpherson's cartoons in the Toronto *Star* suggested they would, but I was struck by the baby-pink quality of his face and the softness of his handshake. I had always been taught fishy handshakes are a sure sign of deviousness, iniquity, immaturity and godlessness.

"Now what's your name?" he asked.

"Fraser. John A. Fraser (I was big on the middle initial in those days)."

"John A., you say! John A! That's a good omen. Olive, meet John A. Fraser. He's going to bring us luck."

Wrong. He went down to even more ignominious defeat than in the previous election. I tend to have this effect on candidates. I have never won my vote in any election — federal, provincial or civic. The last poor sucker I sent to oblivion with my support was Jimmy Coutts.

It was outside the Newfoundland Hotel that I first spied Newman, buckled tightly up inside a dark-blue trench coat and sucking on the ever-present pipe. I had really struck gold: a famous politician and a famous author inside of two minutes. I was just discovering that Newfoundland was an ideal place for trapping Significant People because they were always caught out without the usual defences. I sometimes thought Smallwood and I were in competition to corner the luminaries of the world who found themselves stuck on The Rock for whatever reason. Joey once buttonholed Fidel Castro at Gander and ranted on to him for the better part of a hour before the veteran of years of brutal guerilla warfare had to hide out in the men's washroom at the International Airport to escape Joey's non-stop commentary on "Socialist Newfoundland."

"Why Dr. Castro, do you realize we have here in Newfoundland the very first university in North America to offer free tuition to all its students?"

Dr. Castro demurred. Cuba, the premier was informed, was part of North America and it had a university with free tuition before Newfoundland did.

"Well," said Joey, "then we have the *second* university in

North America with free tuition. We have set the pace, Dr. Castro. You and I. The rest are bound to follow us."

Now where was I? Oh yes, Peter Newman. After we had talked for a few minutes, he told me I could tag along and I spent the next six hours watching this consummate observer dart in and around the Diefenbaker campaign. I watched as he drew out people in conversation and flattered them with his interest, how he handled the difficult and precarious business of taking notes, how he never professed to know very much of anything so that his informants never took anything for granted. In this way he gleaned all sorts of useful trivia and footnote material, which is such a feature of his books. Most of all, I remember his generosity towards me even as he was pumping me for anything I knew. I walked him all over St. John's, especially the harbour area, which he loved. We sat on a bench and discussed my future career in journalism, which was to say he discussed his own philosophy and from this I learned many things that still stand me in good stead.

Most of all he encouraged and I know I was not the only budding journalist he pushed along a particular path. Even today, when he sends an occasional note about this or that article, I remember that talk on the dock bench. "It's the most wonderful profession of all," he said, "because you will never know where it will take you."

MARGARET LAURENCE

Margaret Laurence, CC, BA, FRSC. Author. Born 18 July 1926 in Neepawa, Manitoba. Educated locally and at United College in Winnipeg (now the University of Manitoba). The best of Canada's formidable league of women writers, her books have brought her international fame and also censorship from the school board of her own village of Lakefield, Ontario. She has won numerous awards and honarary degrees and has served as Chancellor of Trent University. Divorced, with one son and daughter. United Church member (with certain reservations).

O nce, when I was happily browsing in Miss Laurence's library on the second floor of her Lakefield, Ontario house, I stumbled across her schoolgirl's copy of *Paradise Lost*. Unlike most people who keep Milton's mighty epic in their libraries, this book really had been read cover to cover and then reread again and again. How could you tell? Miss Laurence likes to write little notes beside certain passages. She is also an underliner. As I leafed through the book, it was easy to see the different coloured ink and pencil jottings. Also, it was possible to see changes in her handwriting over the years, from the still forming script of a teenager, to the firmer hand she eventually settled for.

It was with the juvenile script that she had penned a short, sharp note beside a pertinent passage from the Fourth Book:

> *For contemplation he and valour formed;*
> *For softness she and sweet attractive grace,*
> *He for God only, she for God in him:*
> *His fair large front and eye sublime declared*
> *Absolute rule.*

In blue-black ink, Miss Laurence had written: *"All too typical."*

A few pages later, the commentary was even pithier:

> *Hail wedded love, mysterious law, true source*
>
> *Of human offspring, sole propriety,*
>
> *In Paradise of all things common else.*

"*Ha!*" wrote Miss Laurence. "*I wonder what Mrs. Milton would say*"

"This is revealing," I said with some glee.

"What are you reading?" she demanded, with only the slightest edge of irritation. "Give me that and let's go downstairs for some tea."

She snatched the book from my hands and placed it firmly back in the shelf. I don't know if any journalist has been allowed upstairs since. Future biographers be warned: without a look through that library, you will be lost.

ERIK BRUHN

———————◄ ►———————

Erik Bruhn. Artistic director of the National Ballet of Canada since 1983. Born 3 October 1928 in Copenhagen, Denmark. Studied with the Royal Danish Ballet. Made his professional debut in 1947 with the Metropolitan Ballet in London, England. In 1964 he staged La Sylphide *for the National Ballet of Canada. Resident producer of the National Ballet of Canada from 1973-76. Winner of numerous awards including the* Diplôme d'Honneur *of the Canadian Conference of the Arts, the Nijinsky Prize and the Copenhagen Critics' Theatre Cup. Knight of Dannebrog.*

B ruhn was spared the usual drumhead trial in the Court of Canadian Content when he was appointed artistic director of the National Ballet thanks to the simple expedient of obtaining a landed immigrant card years before, and this in turn had been the result of a long association with both the company and the National Ballet School for which he always showed great affection and concern. He is the best thing that has happened to the company since Celia Franca decided to begin it. Although a perfectionist, and still considered by many to have been the most classically complete *danseur noble* of his age, he retains a penchant for modesty and self-deprecation that makes him as Canadian as Lester Pearson.

I always admired his inability to change his values in the face of seemingly irresistible opportunity or to bow down to the Great Worthies of our times if he didn't think they merited it on a personal level. No prima ballerina was more important to him than a struggling and lowly member of the corps. No mighty impresario, not even the late and hardly lamented Sol Hurok, could make him do what he thought was wrong (and the Hurok organization certainly considered Bruhn a washout in terms of his willingness to go along with some of their outrageous publicity stunts). And not event one of the greatest names in ballet would make him betray, for one second, a valued friendship. On this last point, I can report two versions of the same story from the principal participants themselves: one was Bruhn and the other was Lincoln Kirstein, the lordly father figure of the New York City Ballet and the man who brought George Balanchine to America.

Kirstein is the Diaghilev of our era. His devotion to ballet and his passion to see it become an indigenous part of American life has consumed most of his own personal fortune and all of his adult life. Balanchine created what we now understand to be the distinctive style of New York City Ballet, a style which is always called American when it goes abroad. And, to a very real extent, Kirstein created Balanchine in America. The one couldn't have happened without the other. In addition, this seminal figure is a considerable art historian and critic, and his books on various subjects often enough provide their very definition.

So what was Lincoln Kirstein doing at 3:20 a.m. walking alone along Queen Street East amidst the bleak factory district which separates the Beaches area of Toronto from the downtown core? Good question. We'll start with Version A, as it comes from Kirstein himself.

Kirstein had arrived in Toronto in the fall of 1976 to woo Bruhn away from his seasonal Toronto nook and down to New York to the School of American Dance, the academy which feeds the New York City Ballet. He came with enticements of various sorts, but most of all his very presence was a dramatic signal of the significance Kirstein attached to the appointment. "Toronto is very nice and all that," he said later, "but I didn't go there to see your City Hall, charming building that it is, I'm sure."

Mr. K is not known for small talk or diplomatic courtesies. If he wants something, he goes out and gets it. He appreciates neither interference nor rejection. And he wanted Bruhn. He wanted him so much he was even prepared to include Bruhn's protégé, Constantine Patsalas, at the hard-sell dinner, although he didn't like to be diverted from the task at hand. He was even prepared to listen to Bruhn talk about Patsalas' potential as a choreographer, although the subject bored and irritated him because he had not come to Toronto to look for a budding choreographer, but to nab Erik Bruhn and make him the brightest star in the firmament of his ballet academy, which was — quite frankly — the only important place in the world. And because he wanted that man for his place so much, he was even prepared to go out to Constantine's house in the Beaches and look at his paintings because Erik said they were good.

When he got there and he saw the paintings, Kirstein did what he does as easily as breathing — he criticized them. And he didn't just criticize them, he took such an intense dislike to them that he told the young man he should destroy his brushes, burn his canvases and never let on to anyone else in the whole wide world that he had ever had any pretensions in this area at all. "I've seen paintings on black velvet worthier than those," he said later to me. I gather he said the same thing at Constantine's house.

Let me break here for a moment to go back over these events in Version B, which comes from Bruhn. He was in Toronto very much minding his own business, which was ballet. He was teaching at the National Ballet School and checking out some offerings of the company itself which he had produced for them in the past. He was enjoying himself, his surroundings and his friends. Constantine was his ally and boon companion and was showing undeniable signs of becoming a competent choreographer. When Erik believes someone has talent he pushes it with precisely the same determination that Kirstein goes after what he wants. When the great man called from New York to say that he wanted to come to Toronto to see him, his first thought was, typically, not of himself but of the golden opportunity this might be for young Patsalas. At the very least, the contact would be established and who knows where it might lead in the future. Bruhn knew enough about Kirstein to feel confident that if he liked what he saw, he would support and encourage it all the way.

At dinner, Lincoln had listened appreciatively to the young man's hopes and ambitions and, waylaid by the generally amicable atmosphere, took to Erik's idea that they all go back to Constantine's house and look at his paintings. Although art was only a hobby and not a vocation, the invitation was an act of friendship that Erik thought would be appreciated by all participants. And then this huge and malevolent man started saying atrocious things, wounding the young man as he had never been wounded before and denying him any safe cover from his withering denunciations. Within him, Erik felt a mighty revulsion; a revulsion at someone who had attacked a friend, who had indirectly attacked himself because that friendship was valued, who represented all the pushing and dictatorial tendencies of the people who run ballet companies and think they can order the lives of everyone beneath them, who was betraying all the decent civilities of life and who would make no allowance for youth.

So. So he threw him out of Constantine's house and hurled Danish curses on his head. He shouted at him until the figure of Lincoln was only a tiny dot on a far-away, darkened Toronto street and then he closed the door against the hurt and venom that lurks in this world.

So. So Lincoln tried to save the young man from his folly. If he was potentially as good as Erik claimed, his terrible paintings undermined the point. He should cease and desist. It would have been dishonest to say anything else and for his pains he was shoved out a doorway he never really wanted to cross and sent packing on a filthy, spitting night in a city he knew nothing about. No taxis came his way, so he plodded on towards the big buildings that lay in the far distance. Drunks accosted him at anonymous corners and police were nowhere to be found. During part of the walk, he was sure a mugger was following and stray dogs barked at his heels.

Perhaps I have let Kirstein's grandeur in the ballet world loom too large in my mind over the years, but I am still haunted by the image of him walking along Queen Street East in the early morning. I felt sympathy for him, certainly, and duly commiserated when he recounted his adventures. But most of all I felt pride in Erik Bruhn. He could look good fortune in the face and snarl when it threatened values and loyalties he held to be true. If I was on the board of directors of the National Ballet of Canada today, I wouldn't mess with him lightly.*

* *Erik Bruhn, by rights, should not have been the first to die after I finished this book. He was only 57 when cancer struck him down on April 1, 1986. The bizarre encounter he had with Lincoln Kirstein late one night in Toronto has been left because Erik relished the story himself and it serves as a small antidote to the inevitable iconography that has overtaken him in death. He was a man who had long ago mastered the art of gentle, self-deprecatory humour, which served to reinforce his presiding humanity and warmth.*

G. EMMETT CARTER

His Eminence G. Emmett Carter, OC, MA, Phd. Cardinal-Archbishop of Toronto. Born 1 March 1912 in Montreal, Quebec. Educated at St. Patrick's Boy's School in Montreal and the University of Montreal. Ordained a priest in the Roman Catholic Church in 1937. In 1961 he was appointed Auxiliary Bishop of London, Ontario, and then consecrated Titular Bishop of Altiburo. From 1964 to 1968, he was Bishop of London. Between the ending of that appointment and becoming Archbishop of Toronto in 1978, he performed a wide variety of services in the upper administration of the church. He was elevated to the Sacred College of Cardinals in June, 1979.

H is eminence is no less than his grandeur as a cardinal-archbishop. This is a man who enjoys his high office: its trappings, its power, its potential for leadership, its effect on other people. Of his faith, I can say nothing for I have had no experience of it. His reasonableness in interdenominational dialogue is impeccable and, given a fair chance, his political strategies are not nearly so Machiavellian as his enemies make out. He is a conservative by nature, although much of his earlier reputation was of someone who was a bit of a rebel and shaker. High position in a strict hierarchy, however, has put that earlier reputation into a more logical perspective. He also enjoys the company and hospitality of those who wield power and control vast sums of money. If it is true that it is easier for a camel to get through the eye of a needle than for a rich man to gain entrance to heaven, it is also true that if His Eminence has any say in the matter — and I do not rule it out entirely — then at the Gates of Paradise, needles will stand 60 metres high and their eyes will be sufficiently wide, not just to allow for the passage of dromedaries, but a few Rolls Royces as well.

There was no reason for our paths to cross except the usual haphazard conjunction of arbitrary events. In China I had met Father William Ryan, a notable Canadian Jesuit, who went on to become the Provincial of the English-speaking Jesuits in Canada. The economy has its role in this strange affair too. It was going badly for Pierre Trudeau and, although a devout Roman Catholic himself, radical members of his church's hierarchy were not pleased with what he and his government had wrought. After deliberating for some time on what they saw as the growing economic and social malaise in the nation, the bishops gathered their thoughts and released them in a modest document entitled *Ethical Reflections on the Economic Crisis*, which sent the whole country into a tizzy. Espousing "the preferential option for the poor," the bishops who penned their signatures to this disputatious document immediately accomplished one of their chief aims — to get people talking and debating about the direction society was moving.

His Eminence was caught completely off-guard by this matter and, one gathers, he is not an easy man to be around when he is caught off-guard. His initial reaction was negative and combative, but ever astute to public opinion and the importance of the church's role in that opinion, he deftly took a step and a half away from the immediate fray and announced that the Archdiocese of Toronto would sponsor a non-partisan conference to hear what any interested party, inside or outside the church, wanted to say about the matter. He was going to use his high office to "extend" the debate out of the hierarchical circles and to the broad masses. Because of who he was and what he had said, his actions were immediately suspected. To prove his good intentions he appointed a "listening panel" charged with reporting back what the masses were saying. The chairman was to be the Chancellor of the University of Toronto, the distinguished former Canadian diplomat, George Ignatieff. He was a member of the Russian Orthodox Church. The deputy chairman was Father Ryan, who, as the region's leading Jesuit was no friend of the Cardinal. He was Roman

Catholic certainly, but still an unknown and uncontrollable force. The three lesser members of the panel included a female Jewish psychologist, a Family Court judge and a bemused Anglican journalist from the *Globe and Mail*.

This is an interesting juncture right here! I remember with chagrin all those over-reaching politicians, show-business people and other seekers of the limelight who, when asked about the press controversy their actions subsequently aroused, invariably said: "Had I but known what this was leading to, I should never have . . ." Well, I have to tell you, had I but known what was entailed in accepting the Cardinal's commission, I should never have . . .

In fact, that's not strictly true. I would have preferred not to have gone through what I did (more of which in a moment), but the experience of it was extremely beneficial. It is not often journalists fall victim to the very thing they are accused of causing, and when I now see public figures, of whatever stature, having their protestations laughed at in press conferences and watch how every word of explanation is twisted to mean something else and something invariably more sinister, then my heart goes out to them. For there is in my profession a degree of hypocrisy and a mother-lode of double standards that are pointless to deny. The remarkable thing is how few journalists ever have to experience such things directly, or who even believe they exist. Let me tell you, they do.

Since this yarn has about it the odour of confession, let me start with a *mea culpa*. Journalists should always be alert and wary of whom they associate with. So should tinkers, tailors, soldiers and sailors. At the *Globe* there are and were a number of souls who espoused this wariness to such a degree that they could think of no organization, save their own Guild, and no individuals, save their colleagues and families, with whom they should be associated. When the call from the Cardinal came, the wariness rose up immediately, but then so did the old pernicious ego. I was flattered to be thought fitting by a Prince of the Church. In order to balance the ego and the flattery, I inquired about the responsibilities and encumbrances of the assignment. No money was being offered, not even *per diem* expenses: unlimited supplies of coffee seemed to be the only material incentive. Were we, in fact, really going to be a listening panel, or were we charged with making recommendations out of what we heard? The second option meant that I wouldn't be able to accept. I was National Editor of the *Globe* at that time, presiding over (in theory) political, social and economic news about the country in the main news pages. There was an obvious conflict of interest if my assignment was to offer advice on policy to an institution whose activities passed under my purvue as an editor. No, I was assured, it was just a listening panel. At the most, the panel would be asked to summarize the views of the people we heard.

The matter was put to the Editor-in-Chief and the Managing Editor. They could see nothing wrong with joining under the stated guidelines and the Boss himself agreed with me that it was wrong for journalists to stand above the daily fray, free of any involvement save their professional curiosity — providing the terms of reference did not compromise the paper's integrity.

One of the things not generally appreciated about newspapers by many people outside the business is that a conspiracy is almost impossible to pull off. Now a Tory politician might believe that there is a "left-lib" conspiracy at such-and-such a paper and have his clippings to prove it, but he will never be able to sustain the accusation when faced with the reality. A genuine conspiracy is far too complicated to be effective at a normal newspaper. Believe me, I've tried it.

Here's one small example. I constituted, as National Editor, a conspiracy of one against the then Governor General, Ed Schreyer. I did not think he was the right man for the job and every time I heard him open his mouth in that job I thought he brought ignomy to the office and shame to the land. Clearly, he had been put there by Trudeau and Coutts in their conspiracy to chisel away at the monarchy in Canada. I wasn't overly preoccupied by this thought, but it was there. Still, considering what little regard many Canadians now hold the governor general in and the general indifference Ottawa journalists held for the office, Mr. Schreyer never came off too badly in the *Globe*. Besides, I couldn't control much of his access to the paper anyway: the Picture Editor could do him up proud on the front page, an editorial writer could laud him on page six, the Features Editor could reproduce his speeches on the op-ed page, the columnists could say what they wanted, and because the *Globe* does not specifically cover Rideau Hall, much of his activities were recorded in the paper through the auspices of the Canadian Press, which is religiously neutral.

When Mr. Schreyer's term of office was drawing to its close, however, I saw my chance to strike. It was an obvious time to evaluate what the Governor General had done in office and it was only necessary to find the appropriate journalist. In my devious wisdom, I thought W in the Ottawa Bureau would do a perfect job. W had known leftist and republican sympathies. W was sure to find the office absurd and its occupant even more absurd. And, most of all, W had a nifty edge to his writing: he could bite when he wanted to, and bite deep. So he was unleashed and sent off to do in the Queen's man. I gave him no specific instructions, which would have been counterproductive, but simply waited for human nature to take its course.

When W's article came in, I read it in stupefaction. It was a ringing testimonial to a decent, misunderstood man who had been saddled with a constitutional anomaly of a job and done the best that he, or anyone else, could have been expected to do. His "triumphs" were duly trotted out; his failures were dismissed as part of the limitations of the job; and his enemies — this was the most unpalatable part — were dismissed as a bunch of anachronistic idiots whose knees grew wobbly at the very sight of Prince Albert's portrait. And, of course, I had to run it. Prominently. On the front page. It was a very good piece and I hadn't the heart to employ the then Managing Editor's notorious device to emasculate or destroy articles, known as "Death by a hundred cuts."

It was the same Managing Editor with whom I read the daily news schedule at the regular editorial conference two days after agreeing to accept the cardinal's commission. The daily schedule was divided between the various departments and news desks, and I eventually came to the "city sked" with its usual potpourri of water rates, herpes sufferers, Metro Council debates, drug clinics, Dr. Morgenthaler's latest gambit, "green belt" controversies, Mafioso bakeries and CARDINAL AT-TEMPTS TO SIDE-TRACK CRITICISM WITH HELP OF *GLOBE* EDITOR.

What the hell was this?!

B, the Grand Inquisitor who used to preside over the City Desk, was not smiling at all as he watched me read. He had on his "serious business" demeanour and he knew exactly what he was doing. The Cardinal was right up there on his list of public enemies. The plight of the unemployed, which the commission had a mandate to explore, was nothing in comparison to the shame and ignominy I had brought on the paper for being his dupe. I paid no attention to the provocation, but when I emerged from the news conference I was waylaid by a reporter B had assigned to the story, who wanted to interview me.

"Sure," I said, like the virgin to the artillery captain. "Step into my room."

Was I aware when I accepted this post that some submissions from certain groups would not be acceptable to the Cardinal?

"No," I said in all honesty, "I not only wasn't aware of that, I know it's not true. Anyone can submit anything and he or she will get some sort of hearing."

Well, I asked, if it turned out that some submissions were not acceptable to the Church, would I stay on the panel?

Did I hear the echo of Pierre Trudeau rebelling against hypothetical questions? Did I think this reporter wasn't at all

216

interested in what the commission was actually supposed to be doing? Did I notice that his pen only took down some of the things I said and rested quietly as I tried to "put this matter in perspective"? Did I want to take this reporter and hurl him out of my office because he was cynical, snarling and disbelieving?

Yes, yes, yes, yes and again I say yes. All those things. Instead, however, I put on a mask of utter reasonableness:

"Why obviously, if that ever turned out to be the case I would have to resign the commission. But I know it isn't the case, because it would be counter-productive. Even if the Cardinal wanted to control the public hearings, he would find it impossible because we are organizing ourselves as a wholly independent organization..."

But the pen had stopped writing and the reporter was agitating to get on to the next question.

"Isn't it a fact that these submissions will be addressed to the Cardinal's archdiocesan office and how will you know that you will be receiving everything?"

I didn't answer right away. Instead I looked at him, this little cretin who was 15 years my junior and who flashed the accusing queries at me nearly as well as I used to go after politicians and performing artists who were deemed suitable fodder for media whipping. There was justice in what was happening here. I was not unmindful of it.

"I said, how will you know you have received all the submissions which were sent to the commission when they have to come through the Cardinal's office," he repeated, drumming his pen against his pad.

I knew the appropriate answer. We were to have our own secretary and the mail would be coming directly to her, but I suddenly decided the only way I was going to get this noxious hack off my back right away was to be imperial and pull rank:

"I will take it as a matter of trust that nothing like what you have suggested will happen. If sometime I discover that the trust is not warranted, I will act accordingly. Now if you'll forgive me, I have to get our pages out."

His smile at this line could just as easily have come from sucking the sourest lemon available. I was not confident about the story which would emerge and I was right not to be confident. The article had me threatening the cardinal with resignation if he didn't mend his ways. None of the other panel members were interviewed, the cardinal himself was ignored and the subject of the commission's inquiries was forgotten. I came across like the little lost lamb who had trusted a false shepherd and before 24 hours were out the rest of the Toronto media had a good story, the general thrust being that a sinister mob-like figure disguised as a man of the cloth had inveigled five petty Pooh Bahs to unwittingly help him in his campaign to undermine...what exactly was never clear: church rebels? the unemployed? the City Desk?

It was a two-day wonder, as there really wasn't much to sustain it. My own beloved newspaper, having squeezed the yarn of all its potential dirt, promptly dropped the story. When the public hearings were eventually held months later the same reporter was assigned from the City Desk, but it was clear from his first of two brief appearances that he had more important tasks on his agenda. My ignominy came full circle as I read the accounts of what we were alleged to have heard during three days of non-stop hearings. An entire spectrum of Canadian society had showed that a familiarity with hardship and "bad times" could not destroy its spirit. None of this was reported in my own newspaper. Instead there were criticisms of the location for the hearings and headline coverage of the one submission, by a Protestant clergyman, who questioned our general purpose. One submission out of 243. The reporter didn't even bother coming to the final day.

"The press is a very important institution, Mr. Fraser," said the Cardinal when it was over. "I can't thank you enough for agreeing to join the panel and giving up so much of your valuable time. I hope, at least, it was instructive."

"Very," I said.

And meant it.

Jeanne Sauvé **Edward Schreyer** *Pauline Vanier* **Brian**
elia Franca/Betty Oliphant *John Crosbie* **Northrop**
rad Black *Timothy Findley* **Lord Thomson of Fleet** Z
arles Sewell *Laurier LaPierre* **Stephen Clarkson** *Nan*
erre Elliott Trudeau **Allan Fotheringham** *Richard Sadl*
Davies *John Bassett* **J. Tuzo Wilson** *Donald Jamieson*
wman **Margaret Laurence** *Erik Bruhn* **G. Emmett C**
anier *Brian Mulroney* **James Peterson** *William Davis*
Northrop Frye **Barbara Amiel** *Maureen Forrester* **Rob**
Fleet **Zena Cherry** *Karen Kain* **Joseph Smallwood** E
Nancy Jackman *David Suzuki* **Brian Linehan** *Charle*
d Sadleir *Richard Hatfield* **Robin Phillips/John Hir**
mieson *Herbert Whittaker* **Hugh MacLennan** *Gina*
mett Carter **Telling Tales** *Jeanne Sauvé* **Edward Schre**
Davis *Norman Endicott* **Celia Franca/Betty Oliphan**
ester *Robert Fulford* **Conrad Black** *Timothy Findley* L
wood **Edward John Charles Sewell** *Laurier LaPierre*
han **Charles Ritchie** *Pierre Elliott Trudeau* **Allan Foth**
ohn Hirsch **Robertson Davies** *John Bassett* **J. Tuzo W**
n **Gina Mallet** *Peter Newman* **Margaret Laurence** E
ard Schreyer **Pauline Vanier** *Brian Mulroney* **James P**
Oliphant **John Crosbie** *Northrop Frye* **Barbara Amie**
indley *Lord Thomson of Fleet* **Zena Cherry** *Karen Kai*
Pierre *Stephen Clarkson* **Nancy Jackman** *David Suzu*
an Fotheringham **Richard Sadleir** *Richard Hatfield* R
J. Tuzo Wilson **Donald Jamieson** *Herbert Whittaker* H
rence Erik Bruhn *G. Emmett Carter* **Telling Tales** *Jeann*
mes Peterson **William Davis** *Norman Endicott* **Celia F**
Amiel **Maureen Forrester** *Robert Fulford* **Conrad Bl**
ren Kain *Joseph Smallwood* **Edward John Charles S**
vid Suzuki *Brian Linehan* **Charles Ritchie** *Pierre Elli*
atfield *Robin Phillips/John Hirsch* **Robertson Davies**
taker *Hugh MacLennan* **Gina Mallet** *Peter Newman*

ney *James Peterson* **William Davis** *Norman Endicott* **C**
arbara Amiel **Maureen Forrester** *Robert Fulfo* d Con
erry **Karen Kain** *Joseph Smallwood* **Edward Jo**
man **David Suzuki** *Brian Linehan* **Charles Rit**
hard Hatfield *Robin Phillips/John Hirsch* **Rob**
rt **Whittaker** *Hugh MacLennan* **Gina Mallet**
Telling Tales **Jeanne Sauvé** *Edward Schreyer* **Pau**
n **Endicott** *Celia Franca/Betty Oliphant* **John C**
ford *Conrad Black* **Timothy Findley** *Lord Tho*
ohn *Charles Sewell* **Laurier LaPierre** *Stephen C*
e **Pierre Elliott Trudeau** *Allan Fotheringham* **Richar**
bertson Davies **John Bassett** *J. Tuzo Wilson* **Donald Ja**
eter **Newman** *Margaret Laurence* **Erik Bruhn** *G. Em*
uline Vanier **Brian Mulroney** *James Peterson* **William**
Crosbie **Northrop Frye** *Barbara Amiel* **Maureen Forr**
omson of Fleet *Zena Cherry* **Karen Kain** *Joseph Small*
n Clarkson *Nancy Jackman* **David Suzuki** *Brian Line*
am *Richard Sadleir* **Richard Hatfield** *Robin Phillips/J*
Donald Jamieson **Herbert Whittaker** *Hugh MacLenna*
n **G. Emmett Carter** *Telling Tales* **Jeanne Sauvé** *Edw*
n *William Davis* **Norman Endicott** *Celia Franca/Betty*
en Forrester **Robert Fulford** *Conrad Black* **Timothy F**
h Smallwood *Edward John Charles Sewell* **Laurier La**
n Linehan *Charles Ritchie* **Pierre Elliott Trudeau** *All*
hillips/John Hirsch *Robertson Davies* **John Bassett**
MacLennan *Gina Mallet* **Peter Newman** *Margaret Lau*
Edward Schreyer *Pauline Vanier* **Brian Mulroney** *Ja*
Betty Oliphant *John Crosbie* **Northrop Frye** *Barbara*
nothy Findley **Lord Thomson of Fleet** *Zena Cherry* **Ka**
aurier LaPierre **Stephen Clarkson** *Nancy Jackman* **Da**
eau **Allan Fotheringham** *Richard Sadleir* **Richard H**
assett **J. Tuzo Wilson** *Donald Jamieson* **Herbert Whit**
et **Laurence** *Erik Bruhn* **G. Emmett Carter** *Telling T*